100 MODERN BLUES GUITAR LICKS

Published By GuitarVivo

All Content Taken from Releases at jtcguitar.com

Published by

www.GuitarVivo.com

In partnership with

www.JTCGuitar.com

Transcriptions by Jeff Dafonte and Adam Perlmutter

Edited by Adam Perlmutter

The moral right of this author has been asserted.

Cover Image Copyright: JTCGuitar

Josh Smith Photo Credit: Peter Schepers

Follow Us on Instagram: **GuitarVivo**
Join our Facebook Community; Search: **GuitarVivo – Free Community**

Accessing The Accompanying Media

The bonus files and supporting videos for this book are available free from

www.GuitarVivo.com/blues100

These files are included for free with the book, simply enter your email at the above link. If you encounter a page asking for payment, please double check that you have copied the link correctly.
If the problem persists, email **care@guitarvivo.com**

Feedback and Corrections

At GuitarVivo we pride ourselves on listening and caring for our customer community. We love hearing all your feedback as well as hearing suggestions and ideas for further content and titles. If you would like to provide feedback to us or you've spotted a mistake/typo in the book, then we'd love to hear from you.

For the above or any support issues, please email our customer care department at **care@guitarvivo.com**

Reviewing The Book

Amazon reviews are one of the best ways that you can support the author and this book. If you would like to share your experience and opinions on the book with others, you can do this directly on the Amazon website through the product page for this book or by going to the following link:

www.guitarvivo.com/100review

Contents

Getting the Most from this Book

There are quite a few irrefutable truths when it comes to developing your skills as a blues guitarist; Listen to a lot of blues music, imitate your heroes, play along to records, etc. What those truths all boil down to is four fundamental concepts:

1 – Immerse yourself in the music.
2 - Build practical playing experience.
3 – Build your Vocabulary of riffs, licks and musical ideas.
4 – Develop your musicianship and taste.

With the contents of this book, you'll find a sure-fire way to develop all four of those requirements. What on the surface might seem to be simply a collection of licks, is all the resources you need to create a fully stylized approach to modern blues playing. You'll witness, time and time again, theory, concepts, technique, and more put into real world musical examples. You'll see how your heroes applied their musical taste and style to the blues form, you'll develop your own vocabulary of cutting-edge blues licks, as well as have plenty of opportunity to build practical playing experience by implementing the licks over the provided backing tracks.

As with most lick books, the idea isn't to *complete* the book, or work through it in order like a method book. Each lick represents a window to a different musical world of possibilities, there is no "completing" it. Although you can certainly work your way through the book from start to finish, I don't think that will be the most rewarding or practical approach. I suggest you use this book two ways.

The first is to download the audio, listen through them all and make notes on the corresponding pages if you a) Like the lick and want to learn it, and B) think your current ability will allow you to play it.

Once you've indexed the licks that you want to learn and have an idea of the ones you can learn now, given your current technical abilities, vs the ones you will need to wait a bit for, you can start to cherry pick the lines you digest into your playing. After all, we play what we practice, it makes little sense to practice licks we don't like or want to internalize. From there you can spend a day, week, or month internalizing and creatively applying a single lick.

To get a lick into your subconscious so that you can play it effortlessly is a tall order, not to mention the fact that in improvisational situations you might need to play a variation, segment, or some kind of mutated, adapted version of a lick on the fly. Unfortunately, this process takes as long as it takes, but it will be well worth the wait.

The second approach to this book is to use it as a source of musical ideas for when you need them. Take a good, critical look at your blues playing and look for your problem areas, then find licks that musically address these areas. For instance, struggling to move from the I chord to the IV chord – there's tons of examples with that harmonic movement nailed. Take these examples and dissect and internalize them. This book can help overcome your weaknesses and give you creative, musical material to practice as you do so.

One final thing to note is that we have had to group these licks so that we could present them logically with some sort of theme, however, each of the licks is adaptable to contexts and styles outside of the ones which we have assigned them. A good lick is simply a good melody, and melodies can be applied to any genre or situation once you have sufficient ability. So, don't write off licks in the jazzy section because you don't play jazz. See what you can extract and get your money's worth!

Here is a simple outline for how you might like to approach learning a lick for maximum musical benefit.

1) Listen to the recording of the example.

2) Listen to the recording whilst reading along with the tab/notation.

3) Practice humming, singing, scatting, or clapping along. Start to internalize a feel of the contour, dynamics, timing, and other subtleties of the lick.

4) Ask yourself what you can hear going on and try and verbalise what you find appealing in the lick. For example, you might discover that you're drawn to a lick because of its rhythm. This is a useful realization because it gives you a jumping off point for further exploration.

5) Practice the lick on your instrument. Remember, no matter what tempo you're practicing it at, always express the dynamics, legato/staccato, rhythms, tone, and time-feel as musically as possible. The licks in this book will sound great at a variety of speeds, don't prioritize getting them up to speed before you prioritize making them sound musical.

6) If technique allows, practice along with the recording. Load the example track up and set it to loop in your media player, playing along with every repetition. Trying to identify sticking points and weak areas.

7) In free-time and unaccompanied, practice improvising musical phrases before and after the lick. Create longer frameworks that the lick can exist inside of. The simplest version of this is to experiment with simply tagging on a couple of extra notes before and/or after the lick.

8) Practice improvising along to a backing track and incorporating the lick, segments of the lick, or elements (rhythms, contours, etc) of the lick into your solo.

Now that you have an idea on what to do, go and download the audio and video files from **www.guitarvivo.com/blues100**, and let's get started.

Chapter 1
BLUES SHUFFLE LICKS

With its swung eighth-note feel, the shuffle is one of the foundational rhythms in blues, heard in countless blues and popular songs. In a shuffle, while the eighth notes are usually written is straight, they are in fact played unevenly, at about a 2:1 ratio. Mastering blues shuffles is essential for guitarists of all types, and in this chapter we'll look at a bunch of satisfying variations on the basic pattern.

Lick #1

JOSH SMITH – SHUFFLE LICK 1

In this jazz-informed shuffle lick, Josh Smith plays over the I chord (F9) in the key of F major. The lick starts off on a strong chord tone—the root, F—and incorporates a hefty dose of chromaticism throughout, like the use of a chromatic passing tone (B natural) in the pickup measure, and a repetition of a blue note, the flatted third (Ab), which is resolved by the major third (A). Coming to rest on another strong chord tone, the lick ends on the third.

The groove is just as important as the notes here—play along with the video, and try to copy Smith's laidback time feel. And heads up on the 16th-note triplet in bar 2; that's three evenly spaced 16ths falling on the "and" of beat 2. Be sure to play this hammer-on/pull-off move smoothly and in time.

Artist:	Josh Smith
Key:	F
Tempo:	130 BPM
Level:	6/10
Course:	Rulin' The Blues, Vol.2

Lick #2

JOSH SMITH – SHUFFLE LICK 2

Smith shreds over an F9 in this next jazz-informed lick. He begins by outlining part of an F9 chord on beat 1 (the notes C, Eb, and G), approaching it from a half step below, before elaborating with a bebop-approved line through the end of the second measure. Pay close attention to your right-hand technique here, using whatever pick strokes feel most natural and will allow you to articulate the lick cleanly at tempo.

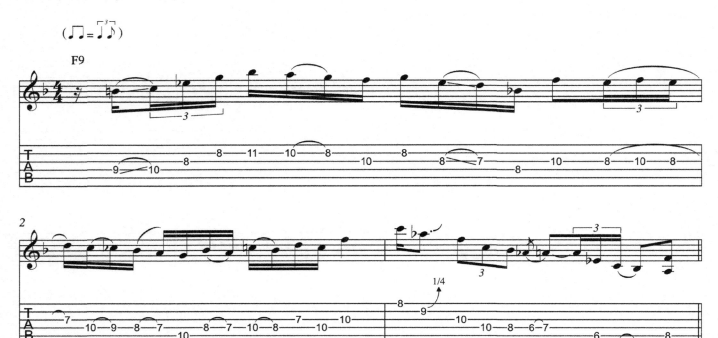

Smith wraps up the lick on a bluesier note—especially courtesy of the quarter-step-bent blue note (Ab) on the "ee" of beat 1 in the final measure. He ends with an A–F double stop, which implies an F major triad in first inversion.

Artist:	Josh Smith
Key:	F
Tempo:	130 BPM
Level:	6/10
Course:	Rulin' The Blues, Vol.2

Lick #3

JOSH SMITH – SHUFFLE LICK 3

Double stops play a starring role in this next lick by Smith, also over an F9 chord. In the pickup bar and the first half of the first measure, note how the upper voice remains a high F, while the lower voice first ascends, then descends chromatically.

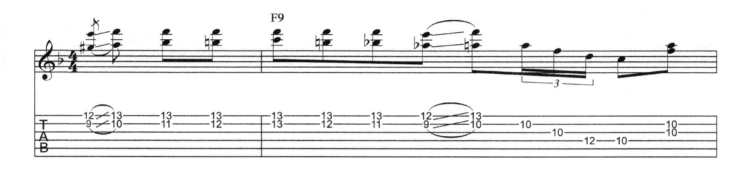

Smith mixes things up in the last two measures. Note the R&B-inspired 16th-note-triplet motif on beat 2 on bar 2, answered by a similar move at a lower pitch level on the following beat. On the last beat of the lick, Smith introduces a double hammer-on, from an F to a Bb triad—the sort of harmonic embellishment that Keith Richards uses all the time in the Rolling Stones.

Artist:	Josh Smith
Key:	F
Tempo:	130 BPM
Level:	6/10
Course:	Rulin' The Blues, Vol.2

Lick #4

Track 4

JOSH SMITH – SHUFFLE LICK 4

Smith takes a more conventionally bluesy approach for the shuffle lick shown below. In the pickup bar, he outlines an F major triad (F A C), approaching the third (A) from a blue note (Ab). After he plays a high F, he hits that note on the string below, for timbral contrast, inflecting it with a stinging vibrato.

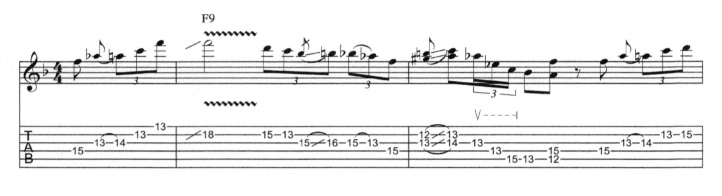

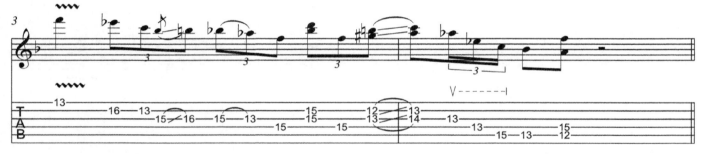

Check out the subtle differences at play when Smith repeats the lick, starting on beat 3.5 of bar 2. Here he outlines an F6 triad (F A C D), rather than F major; he plays the following F on the first string, rather than the second, and adds an eighth-note triplet on beat 3 of the penultimate bar. Avoiding exact repetition is a great way to keep those blues licks interesting.

Artist:	Josh Smith
Key:	F
Tempo:	130 BPM
Level:	6/10
Course:	Rulin' The Blues, Vol.2

Lick #5

JOSH SMITH – SHUFFLE LICK 5

As Smith demonstrates in the lick below, it can be particularly effective to start a blues lick with some "outside" playing—the second beat includes chromatic alterations like the raised ninth (Ab/G#) and raised fourth (B). Also note the angularity of the notes starting on the "and" of beat 3 and extending into beat 4, not to mention the use of palm-muted lower notes that provide textural contrast.

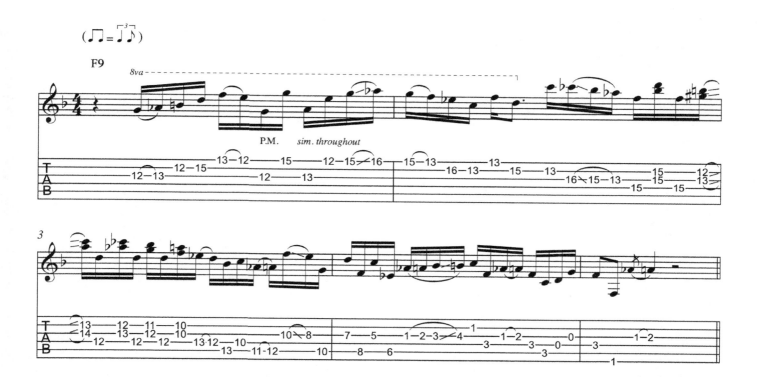

At the end of the second bar, Smith moves on to country-approved chicken picking, traveling down the neck to the open position. In the last measure, he hits a sudden low F on beat 1.5—covering a great range of the fretboard in just a few measures.

Artist:	Josh Smith
Key:	F
Tempo:	130 BPM
Level:	7/10
Course:	Rulin' The Blues, Vol.2

Lick #6

JOSH SMITH – SHUFFLE LICK 6

Revisiting a more traditional idea—but played his own way—here Smith starts off with a pair of octave Fs, sliding them down the neck for striking effect. He then moves on to a series of moves drawn mostly from the F minor pentatonic scale (F Ab Bb C Eb), though, as in his other licks, he does tend to follow the flatted third (Ab) with its major counterpart (A).

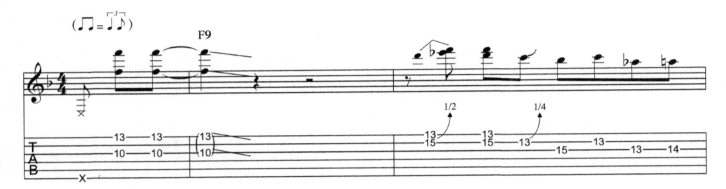

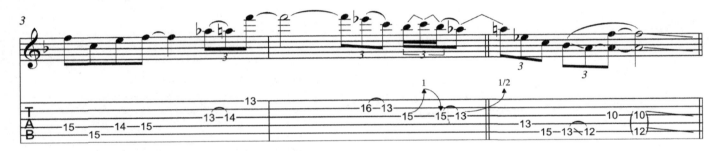

Speaking of major, this is a small but interesting detail—in bar 3, Smith uses the major seventh (E), rather than the expected flatted seventh (Eb), the latter of which is of course a member of the F9 chord. But this "wrong" note somehow works here; it lends a jazzy flavor that somehow does not sound at odds with the underlying harmony.

Artist:	Josh Smith
Key:	F
Tempo:	130 BPM
Level:	6/10
Course:	Rulin' The Blues, Vol.2

ARTUR MENEZES – SHUFFLE LICK 7

In this cool lick in the horn-friendly key of Bb major, Artur Menezes highlights the eighth-note triplets at the heart of the shuffle pattern. Note that two of the triplets include a pair of 16th notes in the middle (bar 1, beat 3 and bar 2, beat 4). If this rhythm is unfamiliar, try practicing the lick very slowly at first, subdividing in triplets, rather than counting in quarter notes.

Choose your fret-hand fingerings carefully here, and always plan ahead, for there are a bunch of sneaky position shifts. At the same time, note the use of quarter-step bends for a bluesy, vocal quality—remember to nudge the string such that its pitch is just slightly raised. And check out the way in which the lick ends on a strong chord tone, the root (Bb), played with strong vibrato technique.

Artist:	Artur Menezes
Key:	Bb
Tempo:	106 BPM
Level:	6/10
Course:	Keep Pushing Blues

Lick #8

Track 8

KIRK FLETCHER – SHUFFLE LICK 8

Based in the more guitar-friendly key of E minor, this shuffle lick by Kirk Fletcher starts off with a strong statement. After sliding into position, Fletcher trills (alternates rapidly) between the Em7 chord's seventh (D) and fifth (B). Be sure to articulate the trill, as shown by the *tr* symbol with a wavy line, with a smooth and rhythmic series of hammer-ons and pull-offs.

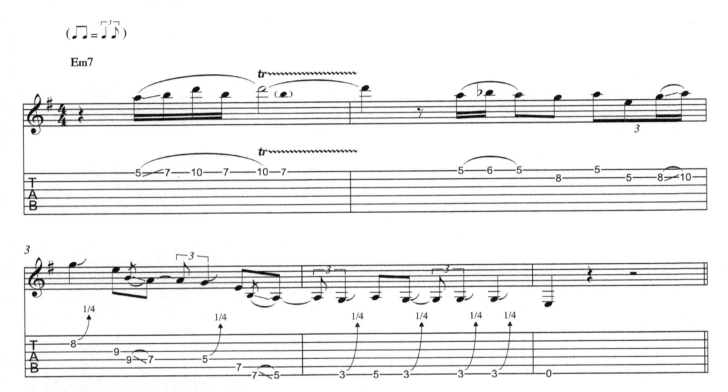

In the penultimate measure, Fletcher settles down into a series of quarter-step bends on the flatted third (G). While these should be easy enough to play, the syncopated rhythms here could prove tricky. If that's the case, try subdividing, noting that the bends on beats 1 and 3 fall on the second eighth note of the triplet, while the bend on beat 2 is on the third eighth note.

Artist:	Kirk Fletcher
Key:	Em
Tempo:	122 BPM
Level:	5/10
Course:	Improvising The Blues Shuffle

JOHN F. KLAVER – SHUFFLE LICK 9

In this shuffle lick in the key of A major, John F. Klaver takes advantage of his Fender Telecaster's biting tone for some whole- and half-step bends up the neck. Pay careful attention to your intonation on those bends, being sure not to undershoot or overshoot.

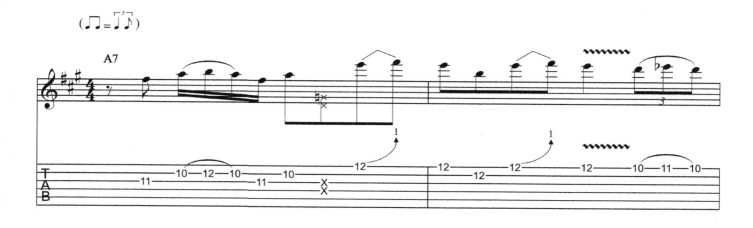

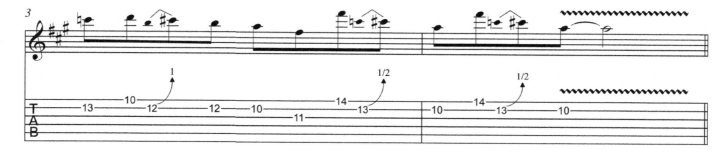

Another thing to appreciate here is the way in which Klaver sticks closely to the A minor pentatonic scale (A C D E G) in tenth position, making the most out of this box on the top three strings.

Artist:	John F. Klaver
Key:	A
Tempo:	132 BPM
Level:	5/10
Course:	20 Blues Shuffle Licks, Vol.1

Lick #10

JOHN F. KLAVER – SHUFFLE LICK 10

We'll close out this chapter with another shuffle lick in A by Klaver. As shown below, this is another excellent idea of how jazz ideas can be used to excellent effect in a straightforward blues context. Klaver starts out the lick by superimposing an Am7 arpeggio (A C E G) on the A dominant seventh chord, leading to a passing bend and release and some chromatic madness in the second measure.

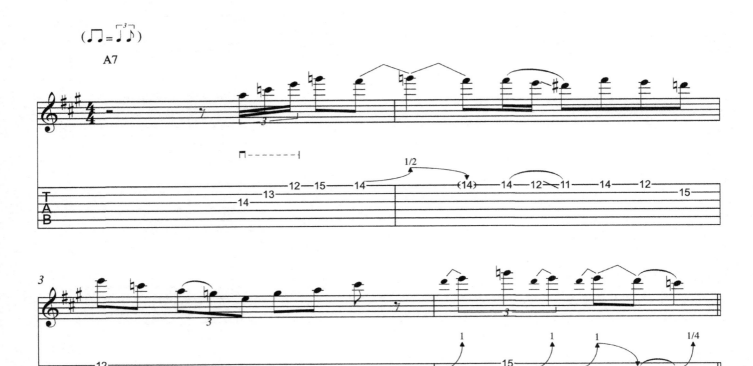

There's a return to Am7 territory in bar 3—this time the chord is played in descending, rather than ascending order, and using longer note values as well—and the lick ends on a bluesier note with a strong series of bends between the A7 chord's fourth (D) and fifth (E).

Artist:	John F. Klaver
Key:	A
Tempo:	132 BPM
Level:	5/10
Course:	20 Blues Shuffle Licks, Vol.1

Chapter 2
BLUES-ROCK LICKS

Blues-rock is a genre that blends the soulful nature of the blues, as well as its structures, with the electricfied nature and instrumentation of rock. As pioneered by guitarists like Jimi Hendrix, Jeff Beck, and Eric Clapton, blues-rock places a premium on heavy, powerful riffs and emotive soloing. Here we will check some examples of modern licks in this style.

AYNSLEY LISTER – BLUES-ROCK LICK 1

The next batch of licks sounds killer on a classic thinline electric like the Gibson ES-335 that Aynsley Lister plays in his video demonstrations. This first one is in E and uses notes from the E blues scale (E G A Bb B D). Lister starts off in a low position on the fretboard, beginning with an attention-grabbing pair of unison Es played on the open first string and at the fifth fret of the second string. In the second half of the lick Lister climbs higher up the neck, ending decisively on the E7 chord's fifth, B.

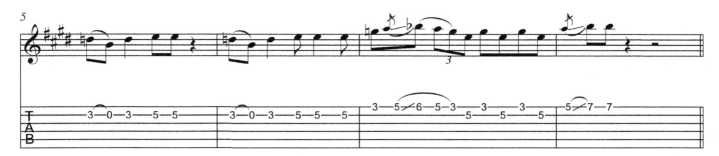

Note Lister's judicious use of space here—remember that the rests are just as important as the notes he plays. Also, observe the guitarist's sense of motific development, whether rhythmic, as in the lone eighth notes on the "ands" of beat 3 in bars 3 and 4, or between phrases, like that first stated in bar 5 and then elaborated upon in the following measure.

Artist:	Aynsley Lister
Key:	E
Tempo:	160 BPM
Level:	5/10
Course:	Twenty Gritty Blues Licks

Lick #12

AYNSLEY LISTER – BLUES-ROCK LICK 2

Perhaps no scale is more closely associated with rock than the E blues (E G A Bb B D), and over an eight-bar E7 vamp, Lister uses this note collection to create a fiery solo replete with bends, legato slides, and eighth-note triplets.

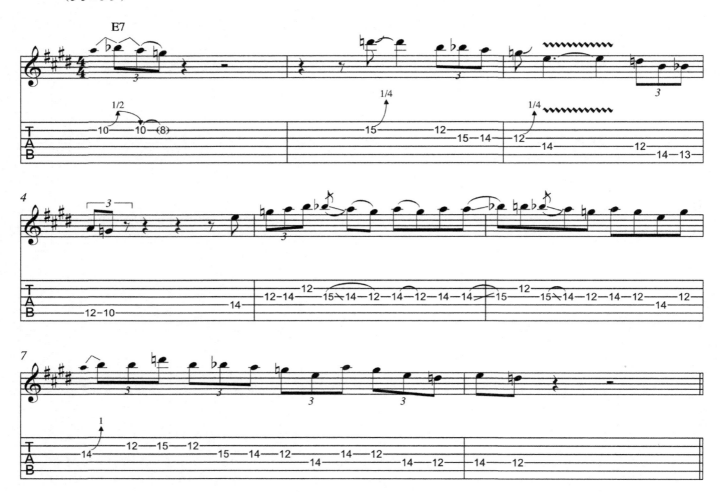

While Lister starts off with a quick bend and release in eighth position, he spends most of the lick in the classic 12th-position shape, dipping down briefly to tenth position to grab the minor third (G) at the top of the fourth measure.

Artist:	Aynsley Lister
Key:	E
Tempo:	160 BPM
Level:	5/10
Course:	Twenty Gritty Blues Licks

Lick #13

AYNSLEY LISTER – BLUES-ROCK LICK 3

Following a slide down on the sixth string, Lister begins this vamp with the same concept as the previous lick—a short declarative statement, followed by several beats of rest, which is an effective means of drawing listeners in while leaving plenty of space for the other instruments in a band setting.

The first several measures are drawn from the E blues scale in open position, making use of the open strings for a biting quality and timbral variety. Note the classic quarter-step bends in seventh position, starting on beat 4.5 of bar 4—a useful device for building excitement in a lick or solo.

Artist:	Aynsley Lister
Key:	E
Tempo:	160 BPM
Level:	5/10
Course:	Twenty Gritty Blues Licks

Lick #14

AYNSLEY LISTER – BLUES-ROCK LICK 4

It's back (mostly) to the 12th position of the E blues scale for a solo over another E7 vamp. Lister starts with a dramatic vibrato and slide up the neck before settling into position. Throughout, he builds rhythmic drive through a series of insistent eighth-note triplets, ending the lick on the E7 chord's flatted seventh (D).

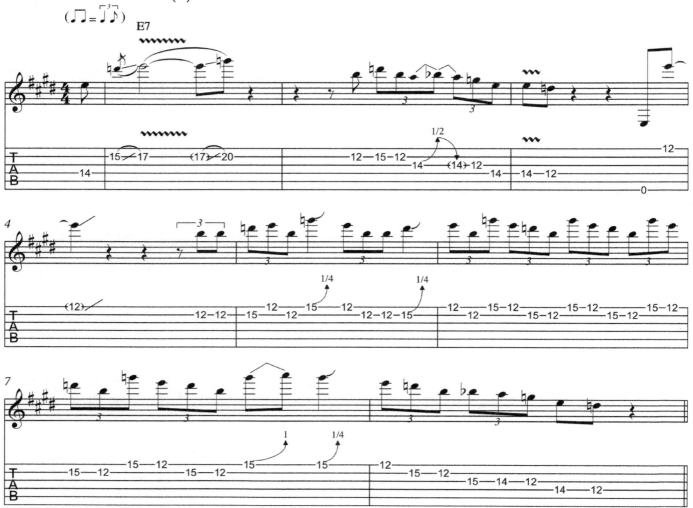

In measure 3, on beat 4, note Lister's use of an exciting leap—he plays a low open E, followed by the 12th-fret E three octaves above, which serves to amp up the proceedings. Try doing the same in your own licks and solos; it's a cinch when you can use a low open string like this.

Artist:	Aynsley Lister
Key:	E
Tempo:	160 BPM
Level:	5/10
Course:	Twenty Gritty Blues Licks

Lick #15

SAM COULSON – BLUES-ROCK LICK 5

In a different direction, this lick by Sam Coulson has a more fusion-y vibe. The figure starts off within the A natural minor scale (A B C D E F G), with the exception of the flatted fifth (Eb) seen in the bend of the pickup bar. In bar 3, there's a hint of A Dorian (A B C D E F# G) through the seventh-fret F#, which Coulson bends up a half step, targeting the E7(#9) chord's raised ninth (G).

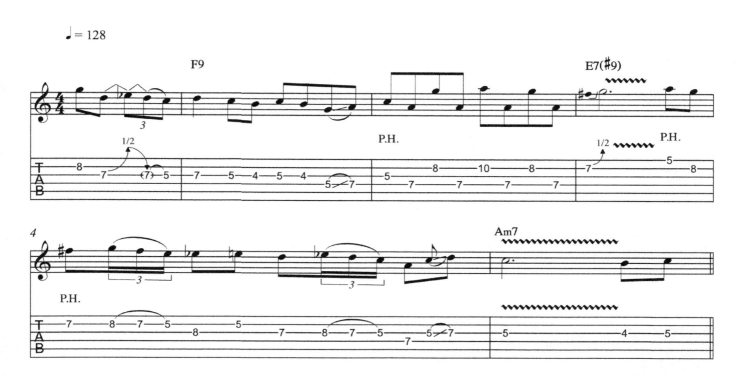

Note that throughout, Coulson makes strategic use of pinch harmonics, indicated as "P.H." in the notation, for ear-catching effects. To play a pinch harmonic, place your pick such that your thumb grazes a string when you pick a note, resulting in a squealing, high-pitched sound.

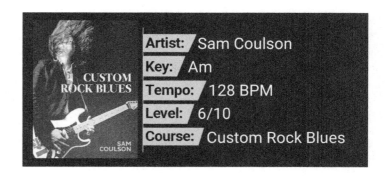

Artist:	Sam Coulson
Key:	Am
Tempo:	128 BPM
Level:	6/10
Course:	Custom Rock Blues

ARTUR MENEZES – BLUES-ROCK LICK 6

While blues and blues-rock styles are typically based on minor pentatonic and blues scales, using a different scale type can be an effective means of adding color and variety. This A-minor lick by Artur Menezes, for instance, is based not on the usual A minor pentatonic scale but the A harmonic (A B C D E F G#), through the use of the raised seventh (G#).

The harmonic minor scale lends a kind of neoclassical feel here, but the half-step bend in bar 2 ensures a bluesy flavor. Be sure to have the harmonic minor scale under your fingers in all 12 keys, so that you'll have it at the ready anytime you are playing a minor-key blues and feel inclined to mix things up.

Artist:	Artur Menezes
Key:	Am
Tempo:	113 BPM
Level:	4/10
Course:	Keep Pushing Blues

Lick #17

ARTUR MENEZES – BLUES-ROCK LICK 7

This lick by Menezes also incorporates the harmonic minor scale, this time in D minor. Menezes kicks off the lick by outlining a jazzy Dm(maj7) chord (D F A C#)—that's a D minor triad (D F A) with a major seventh (C#)—which is found within the D harmonic minor scale (D E F G A Bb C#).

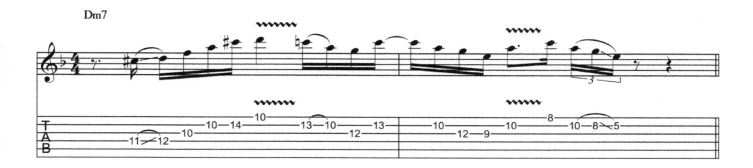

On beat 4 of the first measure, Menezes signals a change of direction through the use of the more conventional D minor pentatonic scale (D F G A C) in tenth position, with the addition of the second (E). Mixing scales in this manner is an excellent way to add depth and sophistication to your blues-rock soloing, while making your music more interesting to the listener.

Artist:	Artur Menezes
Key:	Dm
Tempo:	113 BPM
Level:	5/10
Course:	Keep Pushing Blues

Lick #18

ARTUR MENEZES – BLUES-ROCK LICK 8

In a different direction, Menezes plays the lick below over a bIII–IV–I (C–D–A7) progression in the key of A major. For the bIII chord, he plays notes from the A blues scale (A C D Eb E G), targeting both the minor third (Eb) and major third (E) for a bluesy quality. Over the IV chord in the following measure, he opts to superimpose an Em7 (E G B D) arpeggio, and he then returns to the A blues scale for the I chord.

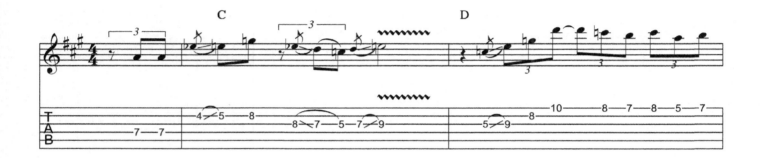

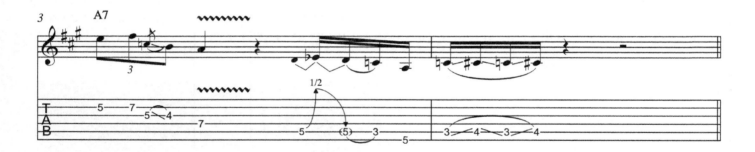

It will take a bit of finesse in both hands to capture the vocal-like quality Menezes achieves here, not to mention the idiosyncratic rhythmic feel, so take things slowly, practicing the lick until you can make your guitar sing like Menezes does in the video.

Artist:	Artur Menezes
Key:	A
Tempo:	113 BPM
Level:	6/10
Course:	Keep Pushing Blues

Lick #19

KIRK FLETCHER – BLUES-ROCK LICK 9

For this blues-rock lick in Am, Kirk Fletcher sticks mostly to the D minor pentatonic scale (D F G A C) over the IV chord (D7), starting off in the tenth position. Beginning in bar 5, Fletcher builds excitement by exploring a 13th-position box of the scale. Then at the sixth measure, he moves to A minor pentatonic for the i chord (Am7), before sliding back down to close things out in the tenth position.

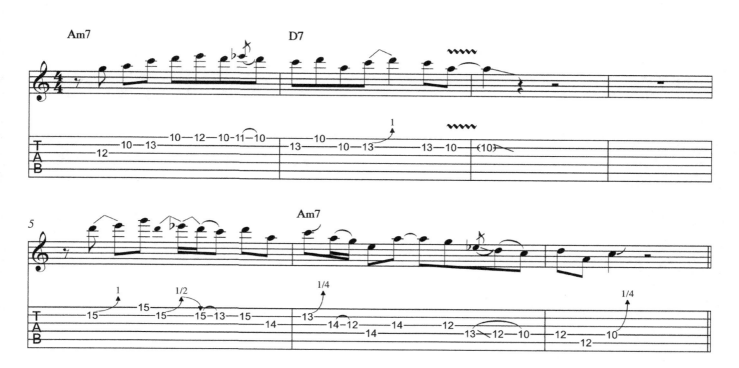

Note the extensive use of rests, from beat 3 of bar 3 through the entire next measure. Again, what you don't play can be as important as what you do play. Be sure to follow Fletcher's example and avoid the temptation to play endless streams of notes in your blues-rock licks and solos.

Artist:	Kirk Fletcher
Key:	Am
Tempo:	165 BPM
Level:	5/10
Course:	Blues: Let's Get Started - 20 Licks

Lick #20

Track 20

KIRK FLETCHER – BLUES-ROCK LICK 10

Let's close out our exploration of blues-rock licks with one more by Fletcher. In the following example, the guitarist sticks to notes within the A minor pentatonic scale, played in straightforward rhythms. But to make things interesting, he plays around with the note order. Check out how in bar 2 he arranges the notes in pairs of perfect fifths, providing a kind of modern jazz sound that is at the same time bluesy.

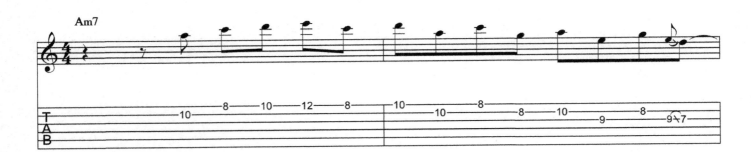

For the IV chord (D7) in the final measure, Fletcher keeps things simple but effective—playing the chord's flatted seventh (C) and then the root, falling squarely on beats 1 and 2. The lesson here is that sometimes the most basic move can be the best choice in a blues-rock lick that is otherwise very active.

Artist:	Kirk Fletcher
Key:	Am
Tempo:	165 BPM
Level:	5/10
Course:	Blues: Let's Get Started - 20 Licks

Chapter 3
SLOW BLUES LICKS

Like the name suggests, slow blues is characterized by its slow tempos, expressive phrasing, and emotional depth. And mastering slow blues is harder than it might seem. It involves a focus on all of the details: nuance, timing, vibrato, and pitch accuracy when bending. In this chapter, learn learn a bunch of different ideas useful for any slow blues form you might find.

ARTUR MENEZES – SLOW BLUES LICK 1

It can be paradoxically more difficult to play slow blues licks than fast ones, as every note is more exposed. This chapter focuses on ideas that will give you the skill and confidence to make your guitar sing in this context. In this first lick, Artur Menezes demonstrates a nicely restrained idea over a moody i–iv progression (Gm7–Cm7) in the key of G minor. Here, Menezes thinks harmonically, playing mainly notes from a G minor triad (G Bb D) for the i chord and targeting the minor third (Eb) of the Cm7 chord.

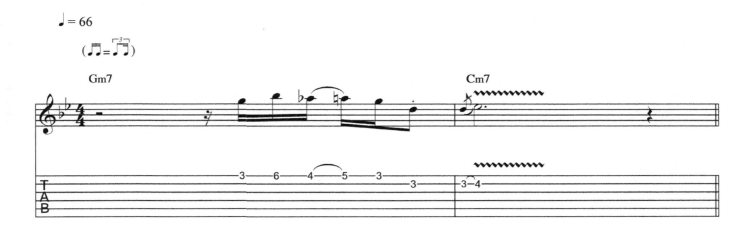

Menezes starts the phrase with a swung 16th-note feel, however, the feel straightens out towards the end of the first bar. He also makes excellent use of tight, controlled vibrato to add expressiveness in the final measure. Make sure that your vibrato here sounds both smooth and rhythmic. It might take a bit of practice to do this with your second fretting finger, as Menezes does in the video.

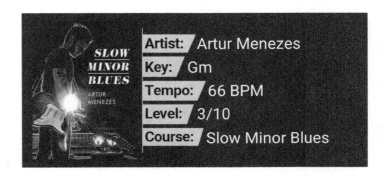

Artist:	Artur Menezes
Key:	Gm
Tempo:	66 BPM
Level:	3/10
Course:	Slow Minor Blues

Lick #22

Track 22

ARTUR MENEZES – SLOW BLUES LICK 2

Here's a jazz-inspired lick that crams a whole lot of notes into a iv–i (Cm7–Gm7) in the key of G minor. Menezes starts the lick by approaching a Cm9 (C Eb G Bb D) arpeggio from a half step below. For the Gm7 chord, he starts with a line that is studded with chromatic passing tones and then wraps things up in a more melodically straightforward way, using notes from the C minor pentatonic scale (C Eb F G Bb).

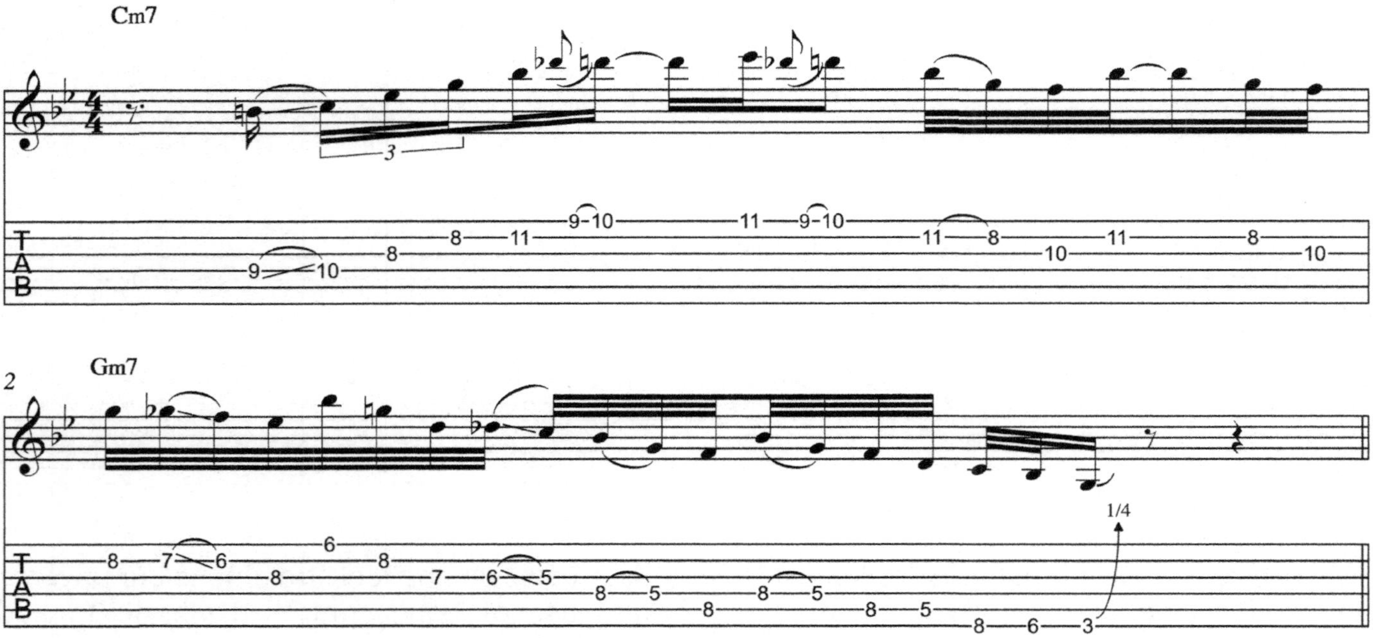

Don't be intimated by the 32nd notes here; just take things slowly and beat by beat. So that you can best understand where things fall on the rhythmic grid, you might try subdividing, counting the notes in eighths or even 16ths, rather than tapping in quarters, as you would with a simpler passage taken at a faster tempo.

Artist: Artur Menezes
Key: Gm
Tempo: 66 BPM
Level: 6/10
Course: Slow Minor Blues

Lick #23

ARTUR MENEZES – SLOW BLUES LICK 3

In this cool variation on the previous lick, Menezes once again begins by outlining a Gm9 chord. This time, in the second measure he shifts the arpeggio shape up five frets for the i chord (Cm7)— a move that lends a nice structure and coherence to the lick.

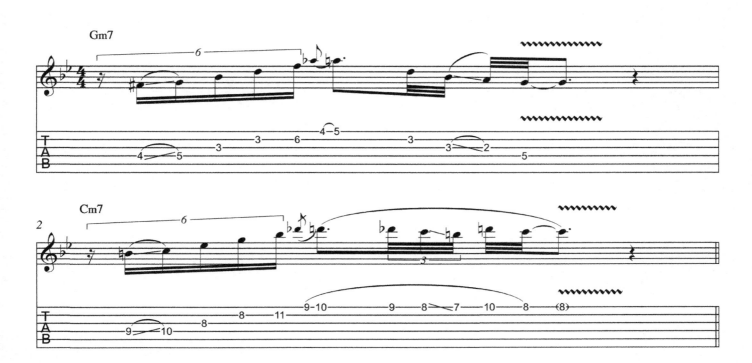

As before, really take your time internalizing the rhythms, which are even more complicated here, making sure that you can accurately count the 16th-note sextuplets. You can think of these as three evenly spaced 16ths per eighth note. At the same time, focus on your fretting fingers as you work out the line from beat 2 of bar 2 till the end—with this kind of legato move, you can create smooth, horn-like effects that sound great in a slow blues setting.

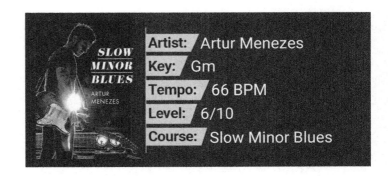

Artist:	Artur Menezes
Key:	Gm
Tempo:	66 BPM
Level:	6/10
Course:	Slow Minor Blues

Lick #24

Track 24

JOSH SMITH – SLOW BLUES LICK 4

So far the licks in this book have been in common, or 4/4 meter. Slow blues pieces, though, are often written in 12/8 time—that's 12 eighth notes per bar. In the following lick, Josh Smith gives a prototypical example of playing in 12/8, which can at first look complicated on paper, but which should be easy enough to negotiate once you get the hang of it.

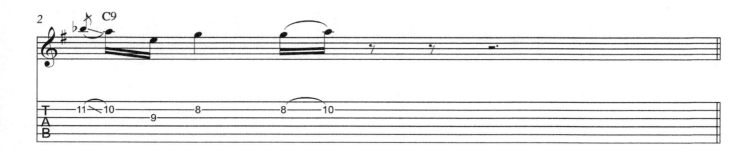

The lick, which is in the key of G major, is based on a box of the G minor pentatonic scale (G Bb C D F) in eighth position. Notice that, while the lick is fiery, Smith gives plenty of room for each of the three phrases to breath—an important concept not just for playing slow blues licks but for soloing in general.

Artist:	Josh Smith
Key:	G
Tempo:	109 BPM
Level:	6/10
Course:	Rulin' The Blues, Vol.3

JOSH SMITH – SLOW BLUES LICK 5

In this variation on the previous example, Smith uses the same progression, tempo, and meter, again using plenty of rests to separate the phrases. Here he tends to target the blue note of Bb, which is both the flatted third of G9 and the flatted seventh of C9.

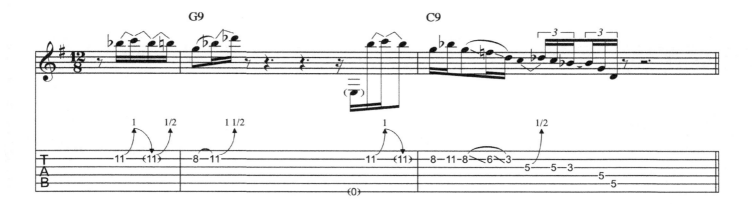

This lick is a great workout for your bending technique, especially those bends and releases in the pickup measure and at the end of the first bar. Note the particularly tricky bend at the top of the first full measure—play the eighth-fret G, then hammer-on the 11th-fret Bb and bend that note up a minor third with either your third or fourth finger, reinforced by your available fretting fingers. If needed, play the 14th-fret Db for reference; that is your target note for the bend.

Artist:	Josh Smith
Key:	G
Tempo:	109 BPM
Level:	6/10
Course:	Rulin' The Blues, Vol.3

JOSH SMITH – SLOW BLUES LICK 6

In this last slow blues lick in G, Smith plays his most intricate variation yet, filled with 16th-note triplets throughout. If this rhythm gives you trouble, try setting a metronome to an eighth-note pulse in 12/8 time, and count/feel three evenly spaced notes on each beat.

Note the classic move in the second measure, where Smith plays a series of broken major sixths that travel down chromatically. Smith ends the lick by breaking up the texture through a pair of stabs on the top notes of a C9 (C E G Bb D) voicing—a good way to avoid sonic clutter in a band with a bassist covering the low end and a keyboardist also adding harmonic information.

Artist:	Josh Smith
Key:	G
Tempo:	109 BPM
Level:	6/10
Course:	Rulin' The Blues, Vol.3

JOHN F. KLAVER – SLOW BLUES LICK 7

Here's another lick in 12/8 time, this time for use on the IV chord (C9) of a slow blues in the key of G major. If you have mastered the previous licks in 12/8 time, then it should be easy enough to count and feel this example, but remember to learn the lick bit by bit if any of the spots prove difficult in terms of timing.

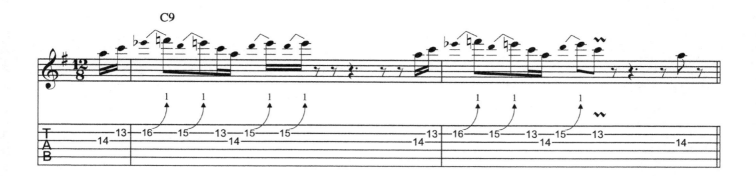

The real trick of this lick is to accurately play the bends, as Josh F. Klaver does so smoothly on his Gibson Les Paul–style guitar in the video. At the beginning of each full measure, you'll need to grab the C9 chord's flatted third (Eb) at the 16th fret of string 2 and bend it up a whole step, to F. Then, rapidly move down to the 15th-fret D on the same string, again bending the note up a half step, to the chord's third (E).

Artist:	John F. Klaver
Key:	G
Tempo:	158 BPM
Level:	5/10
Course:	Blues Foundation

AYNSLEY LISTER – SLOW BLUES LICK 8

Here's a moody slow blues passage in the key of B minor and in 6/8 time—that's six eighth notes per measure, counted in the same way as half a measure of 12/8. Aynsley Lister starts off the lick with an insistently repeated dyad that implies a Bm7 chord (B D F A). Note the use of tremolo here—as indicated by the slanted diagonal lines, pick these double stops in a rapid, alternating down-up pattern, making sure to keep things rhythmic.

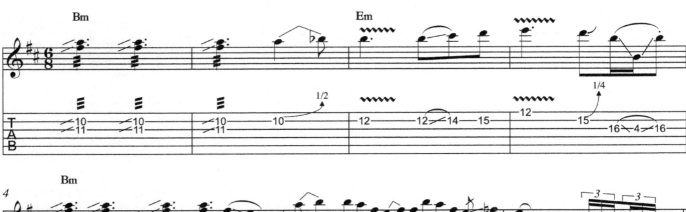

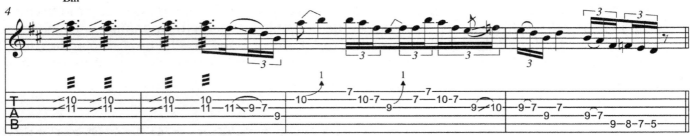

The lick ends with a phrase drawn from the B blues scale (B D E F F# A) in seventh position, dipping down to the fifth fret to come to rest on a strong chord tone, the minor third (D) of Bm.

Artist:	Aynsley Lister
Key:	Bm
Tempo:	134 BPM
Level:	5/10
Course:	20 Blues Breaking Licks

DENNY ILETT – SLOW BLUES LICK 9

Moving back to the major mode, here is a jazzy passage played over the first five measures of the 12-bar blues in G. Note how Denny Ilett targets certain chord tones to bring the changes out, for instance, hitting the major third (E) of the C9 chord at the top of bar 2 and the doubly flatted seventh (Bb) of the C#°7 on the third beat of the same measure.

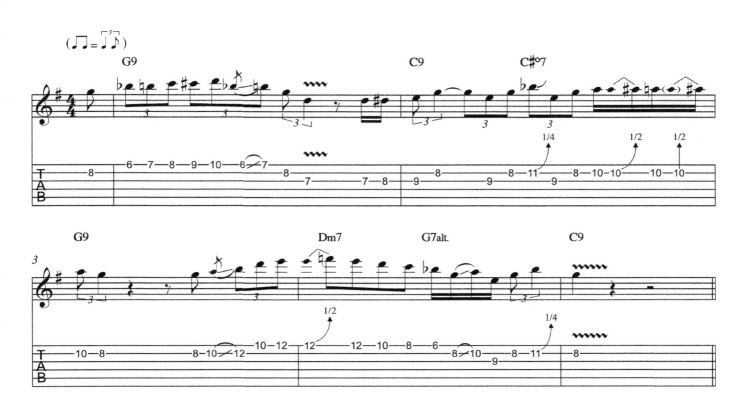

But of course, just as important as the notes—if not more so—is Ilett's impeccably laidback time feel. Be sure to play along with the video in order to match it as closely as possible, as this sort of vibe is essential to slow blues soloing.

Artist:	Denny Ilett
Key:	G
Tempo:	90 BPM
Level:	5/10
Course:	Fifty Shades of Blues, Vol.2

DENNY ILETT – SLOW BLUES LICK 10

Ilett takes an even jazzier approach in this next example, which is also in the key of G major. He uses a handful of chromatic and alterered notes on each dominant chord (C9 and E7alt.), and an ascending C#°7 arpeggio for the chord in the second measure.

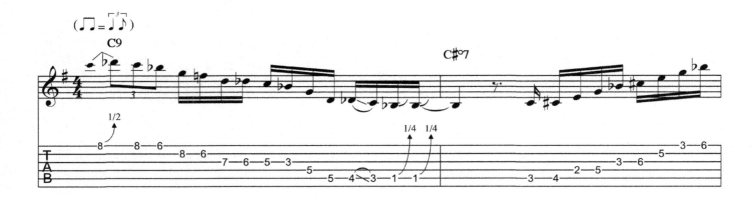

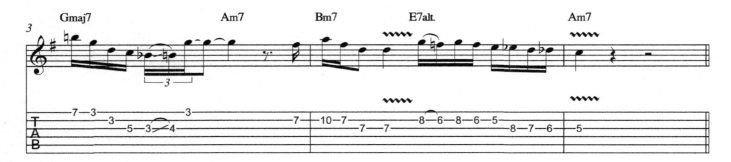

For the other chords, Ilett uses more straightforward note choices, for example, sticking closely to a G major arpeggio (G B D) for the Gmaj7 chord (G B D F#) and playing a descending Bm7 (B D F A) arpeggio, minus the root note (B). He brings the lick to a close with the minor third (C) of the Am7 chord (A C E G), rendered with expressive vibrato.

Artist:	Denny Ilett
Key:	G
Tempo:	90 BPM
Level:	6/10
Course:	Fifty Shades of Blues, Vol.2

Chapter 4
MINOR BLUES LICKS

In the blues, there is often tension between the major and minor modes. While they might include lots of flatted thirds, many blues songs are based on the major 12-bar form. However, blues can be in strictly minor keys, and this chapter focuses on that particular context through a bunch of useful licks.

.

Lick #31

JAKE WILLSON – MINOR BLUES LICK 1

This first minor blues lick, played by Jake Willson, is in G minor and includes the i (Gm7), v (Dm7), and iv (Cm7) chords, giving you something to build on for playing the 12-bar blues in that key.

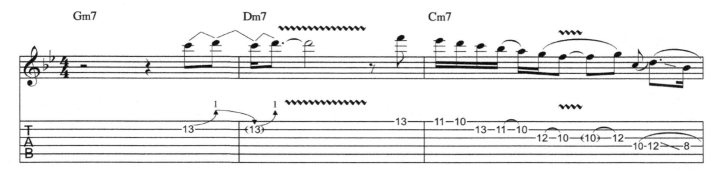

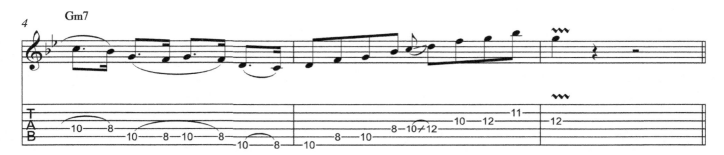

After starting with a declarative bend-release-bend that leads into a vibrato-inflected root note (D) on the Dm7 chord, Willson negotiates the iv chord with notes from the C Dorian mode (C D Eb F G A Bb), opting for the more traditional choice of the G pentatonic minor scale (G Bb C D F) for the i chord in the last several measures. Note how his use of legato technique (pull-offs, hammer-ons, and slides) lends a smooth and singing quality.

Artist:	Jake Willson
Key:	Gm
Tempo:	88 BPM
Level:	5/10
Course:	Blues Soloing Masterclass - Beginner

Lick #32

JAKE WILLSON – MINOR BLUES LICK 2

For this next example, also in the key of G minor, Willson takes an interesting approach. Over the v–iv–i (Dm7–Cm7–Gm7) progression, he draws mostly from the G blues scale (G Bb C Db D F). The main exception is the chromatic motif that begins on the downbeat of the first full measure and extends into the next beat.

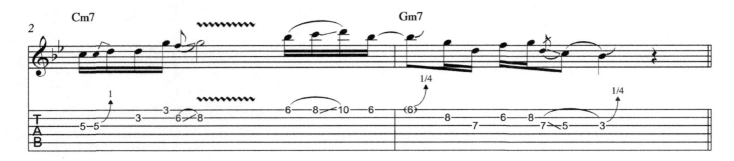

Note how on beat 2 of the second measure, Willson slides out of the scale in third position before shifting up again on beat 4. These moves not only build the intensity of the lick, they add some cool legato sounds and are quite fun to play.

Artist:	Jake Willson
Key:	Gm
Tempo:	88 BPM
Level:	5/10
Course:	Blues Soloing Masterclass - Beginner

Lick #33

JAKE WILLSON – MINOR BLUES LICK 3

Willson takes a decidedly jazzy approach in this lick based on a v–iv–I (Dm7–Cm7–Gm7) progression in G minor. He starts off by outlining a Dm7 chord (D F A C), then over the Cm7 chord, he gets into adventurous modern territory rife with chromatic passing tones.

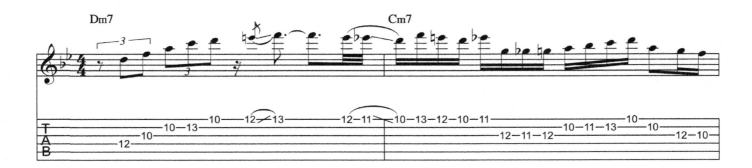

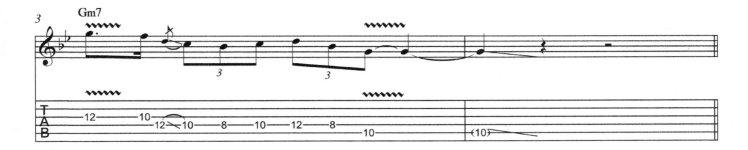

When he arrives at the i chord in the third measure, Willson settles down into a bluesier mode, closing out the lick with a line drawn from the G minor pentatonic scale (G Bb C D F). Note how athletic this passage is; Willson avoids the usual box formation to give the phrase a greater sense of movement and excitement.

Artist:	Jake Willson
Key:	Gm
Tempo:	88 BPM
Level:	6/10
Course:	Blues Soloing Masterclass - Beginner

Lick #34

JAKE WILLSON – MINOR BLUES LICK 4

In this G minor groove, Willson sets things up with notes from the G minor pentatonic scale, starting in third position, then moving up to a box in the sixth position. Things get a bit tricky starting with the series of bends and releases at the end of the first measure—pay close attention to your intonation and timing here.

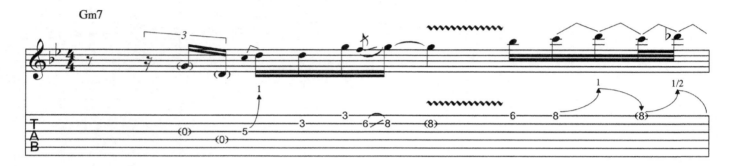

Harder still is the passage over the iv chord (Cm7). An impeccable legato technique is needed here in order to emulate Willson's liquid sense of phrasing. Make sure that all of the hammer-ons, pull-offs, and slides sound and equal volume, and also fall in the right place on the rhythmic grid. Once you've got it down, this sort of legato approach can provide great expressiveness to your playing.

Artist:	Jake Willson
Key:	Gm
Tempo:	88 BPM
Level:	5/10
Course:	Blues Soloing Masterclass - Beginner

Lick #35

JAKE WILLSON – MINOR BLUES LICK 5

In a more straightforward vein, here's a classic and useful lick based entirely on the G blues scale in third position. A judicious use of mixed bends—quarter, half, and whole step—lends just the right amount of bluesy inflections, as does the use of subtle vibrato on the root note (G) in the final measure.

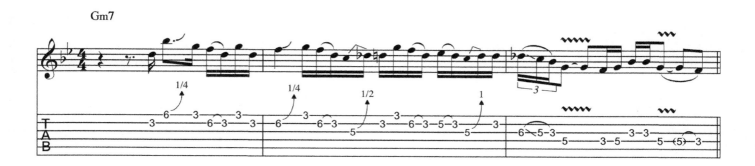

Note the fleeting appearance of the E on beat 4 of measure 2, which quickly hints at the G Dorian mode (G A Bb C D E F). When soloing using a minor pentatonic or blues scale, try doing the same, selectively adding the raised sixth scale degree for a bit of melodic spice.

Artist:	Jake Willson
Key:	Gm
Tempo:	88 BPM
Level:	7/10
Course:	Blues Soloing Masterclass - Beginner

Lick #36

KIRK FLETCHER – MINOR BLUES LICK 6

Kirk Fletcher makes the most of the E minor pentatonic scale (E G A B D), with the occasional flatted fifth (Bb) grace note in this iv–i (Am7–Em7) progression in the key of A E minor. Fletcher starts with a ninth position box of the scale, working his way down to the fifth position and ending on the Em7 chord's seventh (D).

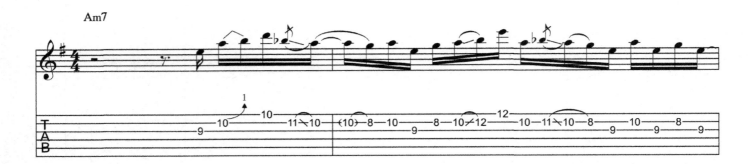

Note the use of palm muting on select sixth-string notes—a good way to add definition and textural contrast to any lick or solo, minor blues or otherwise.

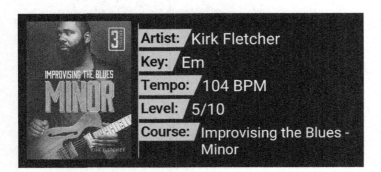

Artist:	Kirk Fletcher
Key:	Em
Tempo:	104 BPM
Level:	5/10
Course:	Improvising the Blues - Minor

Lick #37

KIRK FLETCHER – MINOR BLUES LICK 7

For this midtempo groove in A minor, Fletcher mixes up A minor pentatonic ideas with some modern jazz concepts, like the chromatic cell on beat 4 of the first full measure. Though the harmonic progression is fairly involved, it is clear that Fletcher is thinking less in terms of making the changes than creating beautifully flowing melodic lines.

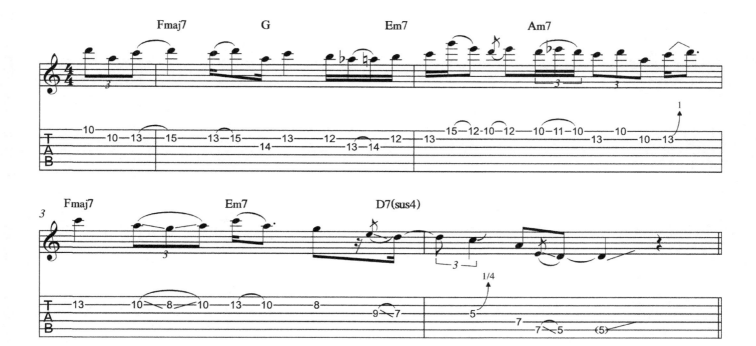

With its 16th-note syncopations and occasional triplets, this lick might prove a bit rhythmically tricky. If you find yourself stumbling over the rhythms, then just set aside your guitar and try counting along with a metronome, subdividing if needed.

Artist:	Kirk Fletcher
Key:	Am
Tempo:	120 BPM
Level:	5/10
Course:	Improvising the Blues - Minor

KIRK FLETCHER – MINOR BLUES LICK 8

You don't have to blow fancy lines over a complex jazz progression, as Fletcher demonstrates in this cool minor lick in the key of C minor. In the first two bars, rather than negotiate the chord changes of the line cliché (Cm–Cm[maj7]–Cm7–Cm6), he plays notes from the C minor pentatonic scale (C Eb F G Bb).

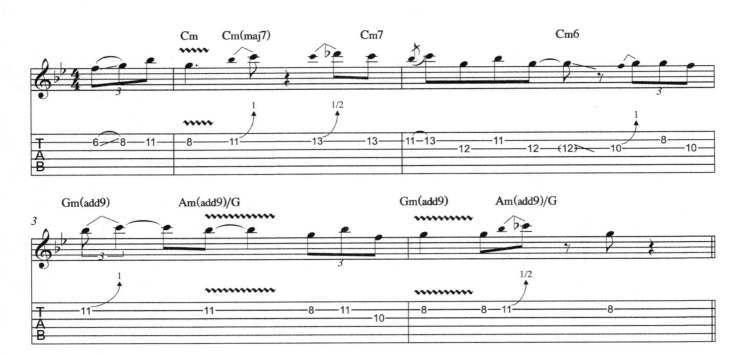

The same goes for the progression of the last two bars (Gm[add9]–Am[add9]), where the notes within the scale make a strong statement—even if the Bb technically clashes with the Am(add9)/G chord. Remember, the wrong note can often be right if played with conviction, like Fletcher does here.

Artist:	Kirk Fletcher
Key:	Am
Tempo:	120 BPM
Level:	5/10
Course:	Improvising the Blues - Minor

Lick #39

JOSH SMITH – MINOR BLUES LICK 9

Josh Smith tips his hat to the legendary jazz guitarist Wes Montgomery in this cool lick in the key of C minor. In the first bar, he uses octaves to outline the notes of a Dm7 chord (D F A C), adding further embellishments in the following measure. He ends the lick strongly, sliding into octaves on the Cm7 chord's root note (C), approaching them by half step. Though not necessarily as bluesy as the other minor licks in this chapter, Smith does achieve a bluesy feeling with the chromatic grace notes throughout.

In terms of fingerings, use your fourth and first fingers to play the octaves on string pairs 1–3 and 2–4 and your third and first for those on 3–5 and 4–6.Montgomery picked with his thumb, rather than a pick, and Smith does the same in the accompany video. However, feel free to use a plectrum if that feels most natural. Whatever picking approach you chose, just remember to mute the middle string of each octave with the underside of your first fretting finger, as it's important to avoid sounding those unwanted notes.

Artist:	Josh Smith
Key:	Cm
Tempo:	127 BPM
Level:	6/10
Course:	Blues Grab Bag, Vol.2

Lick #40

Track 40

JOSH SMITH – MINOR BLUES LICK 10

In this chapter's final minor blues lick, Smith plays a line of insistent 16th-note triplets over a i–vi (Cm7–Gm7) progression in the key of C minor. He starts off sticking mostly to the chord tones of a C minor triad (C Eb G), but beginning halfway through the Cm7 measure, he achieves a bluesy feel by choosing notes from the C minor pentatonic scale. Smith ends the lick with a beautiful, singing vibrato on the root note (G)—an excellent way to bring a blues phrase to a close.

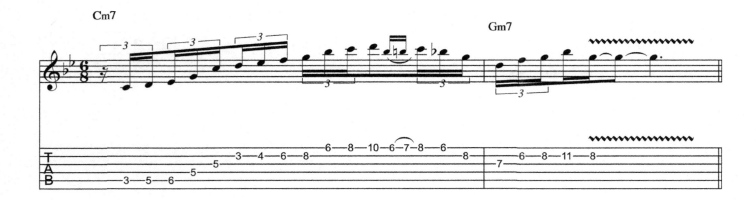

In terms of the picking hand, Smith plays this lick using a majority of downstrokes, which provide a robust tone. However, you should experiment to find the approach that is best for you—alternate or economy should also work well, as long as the picking is super clean.

Artist:	Josh Smith
Key:	Cm
Tempo:	127 BPM
Level:	6/10
Course:	Blues Grab Bag, Vol.2

Chapter 5
JAZZY BLUES LICKS

Whether as a form or a language, the blues is inseparable from jazz and vice versa; it's helpful for any blues guitarist to have a bunch of jazz licks at their disposal, and the opposite is also true. In this chapter we'll look at the blues through a jazz lens, with licks based on everything from Gypsy to modern jazz.

OLLI SOIKKELI – JAZZY BLUES LICK 1

The blues and jazz are in many ways inextricably linked. Blues, with its expressive and emotive style, served as a foundational influence for jazz, influencing its melodic structures and improvisational nature. In turn, jazz expanded upon the blues by incorporating complex harmonies, syncopated rhythms, and varied instrumentation. Both genres evolved alongside each other, with jazz artists often incorporating blues elements into their improvisations, fostering a dynamic interchange that has shaped the landscape of American music.

The 12-bar form used in countless blues songs is also one of the most common forms in jazz, and the next handful of ideas are based on full 12-bar solos. In this first example, Olli Soikkeli plays a Gypsy jazz chorus on the blues form in the key of C, with nonstop eighth-note triplets at a jaw-dropping pace.

While it might seem that there is a lot of information to learn to play this solo, its repetitive nature means that once you have learned the first measure, the rest should fall into place. Notice, for instance, that the only difference between the C6/C7 and F6 measures is that the first note is different—E on the I chord and Eb on the IV.

Of course, the trick to perfecting this solo is playing it at tempo. Remember, you have to walk before you can run, so it might be beneficial to learn this at half speed, gradually increasing the tempo until you can cleanly play along with the video.

Artist:	Olli Soikkeli
Key:	C
Tempo:	232 BPM
Level:	8/10
Course:	20 Gypsy Jazz Licks

OLLI SOIKKELI – JAZZY BLUES LICK 2

Just as the previous chorus included repeating melodic cells, this example makes the most of a single dominant seventh chord shape for both the I (C7) and IV (F7) chords—and one you might not have previously encountered. While voicings like this sound particularly good on a proper Gypsy jazz guitar, with its rhythmic bark, they can be useful to add variety to any style of music, on any type of guitar.

Once you have the chord shape in your muscle memory, try playing along with the video, trying to copy Soikkeli's exuberant swing feel. Note the use of muted chords throughout, as indicated by the Xs in notation—remember to release pressure on your fretting fingers to make a percussive sound. Also note the chromatic chordal move between the I and IV chords, starting in bar 4 and ending at the top of the following measure. This happens to also be a classic jazz ending, and a good move in general to have in your tool kit.

Artist:	Olli Soikkeli
Key:	C
Tempo:	232 BPM
Level:	8/10
Course:	20 Gypsy Jazz Licks

OLLI SOIKKELI – JAZZY BLUES LICK 3

The following chorus, another 12-bar blues, starts off with the exact same pickup measure as Lick 41—a common Gypsy jazz move—but takes a different approach starting in the first measure. Here, a five-note sequence (Eb D C Bb A) is played in consecutive eighth notes, creating a compelling rhythmic displacement as the sequence is repeated on different beats. The Eb over the I chord provides a nice bluesy quality.

The rest of the solo is less repetitive than the previous two choruses. Some highlights include syncopated arpeggios (bars 5–6, etc.) and swinging double stops (bars 7–9). After you have learned this chorus in its entirety at tempo, be sure to memorize the phrases that you find most compelling. Transpose them to other keys, and do not be afraid to pull them out at that next blues jam.

Artist:	Olli Soikkeli
Key:	C
Tempo:	232 BPM
Level:	7/10
Course:	20 Gypsy Jazz Licks

DENNY ILETT – JAZZY BLUES LICK 4

Here's a fusion type of lick that explores the bluesier side of jazz. Based on a i–iv–v–i progression (Am7–Dm7–Em7–Am7) in the key of A minor, the example shows the diversity of the minor pentatonic scale, and how it can be used to guide a solo, as opposed to thinking strictly in terms of chord tones.

Key to mastering this lick is copping Ilett's masterly sense of phrasing, and the unpredictable speechlike rhythms captured here in notation. After you've got this one down, try improvising some of your own licks over the progression, imagining your lines as words and sentences.

Artist:	Denny Ilett
Key:	Am
Tempo:	95 BPM
Level:	6/10
Course:	20 Melodic Jazz Blues Licks

62

Lick #45

DENNY ILETT – JAZZ BLUES LICK 5

This lick is based on the same chord progression as the previous example, but here Ilett takes a decidedly jazzier approach. In the first bar, he begins by outling the upper notes of an Am9 chord (A C E G B), and he then proceeds to draw from the A Dorian mode (A B C D E F# G) throughout the measure. To keep things bluesy, he chooses notes from the A minor pentatonic scale in the next measure.

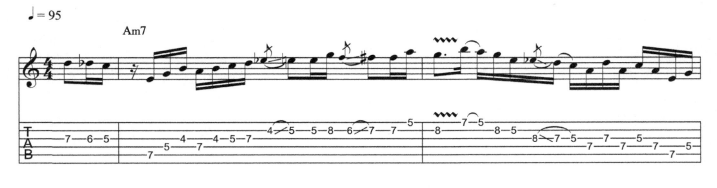

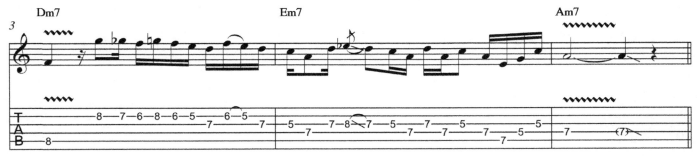

Switching back to a jazzy vibe in bar 3, Ilett targets the Dm7 chord's minor third (F) at the top of the measure, and then he spins a chromatic line before switching back to minor pentatonic for the Em7 chord, landing on the Am7 chord's root note (A) to close out the lick. The takeaway here is that it can be interesting and effective to mix scales and modes in this manner.

Artist:	Denny Ilett
Key:	Am
Tempo:	95 BPM
Level:	6/10
Course:	20 Melodic Jazz Blues Licks

DENNY ILETT – JAZZY BLUES LICK 6

Here is another example of mixing different approaches to create a compelling jazz-blues lick over the established chord progression in A minor. The lick starts out with some nice motific development in the first measure, as Ilett elaborates on the G-to-A-to-C move seen in the pickup measure. His use of the A blues scale (A C D Eb E G) in the second measure ensures a bluesy vibe.

When Ilett gets to the iv chord (Dm7) in bar 3, he plays around with some chromaticism, and then he sticks mostly to the A minor pentatonic scale for the Em7 chord in the following measure. Note the use of sliding sixths at the end of that bar; this device can wow listeners when skillfully deployed.

Artist:	Denny Ilett
Key:	Am
Tempo:	95 BPM
Level:	7/10
Course:	20 Melodic Jazz Blues Licks

Lick #47

DANIELE GOTTARDO – JAZZY BLUES LICK 7

In this lick, based on the first three bars of the 12-bar blues in F, Daniele Gottardo plays a swinging single-note line inspired by the jazz legend Charlie Parker. In the first bar, Gottardo negotiates the I chord starting on the third of an Fmaj7 arpeggio (F A C E G). Likewise, in the second measure he uses a Bbmaj9 arpeggio (Bb D F A C) over the IV chord, even though the backing track contains a dominant seventh chord, creating an interesting tension.

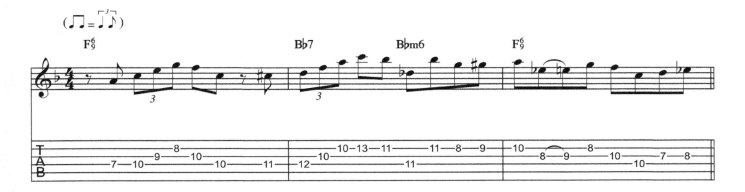

Also note the use of chromatic approach notes, like the C# at the end of bar 1 that precedes the D at the top of the next measure, and chromatic passing tones like the G–G#–A move that starts on beat 4 of the second measure. Moves like these are essential to the bebop language and, as Gottardo demonstrates here, fall nicely under the fingers on the fretboard.

Artist:	Daniele Gottardo
Key:	F
Tempo:	130 BPM
Level:	5/10
Course:	20 Licks to Expand Your Jazz Blues

DANIELE GOTTARDO – JAZZY BLUES LICK 8

In another Charlie Parker–inspired lick, Gottardo negotiates the dominant seventh chords with tense alternations like the raised ninth (Ab/G#), flatted ninth (Gb), and flatted 13th (Db) on the F7 chord—all while maintaining the impeccable sense of swing that is at the heart of the jazz-blues language.

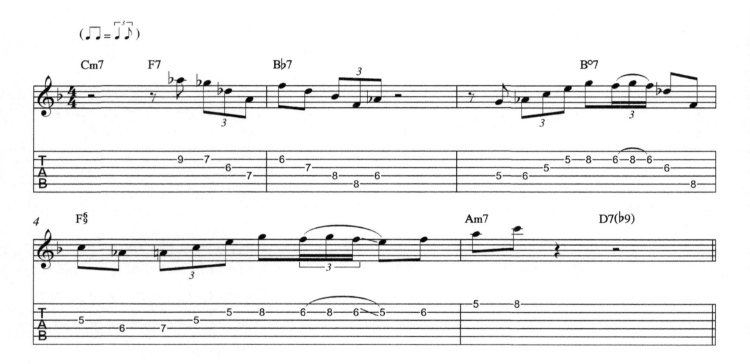

Note the generous sense of space between the phrases, and the ways in which each one falls neatly in position on the fretboard, even though lines like these were originally played on the saxophone.

Artist:	Daniele Gottardo
Key:	F
Tempo:	130 BPM
Level:	5/10
Course:	20 Licks to Expand Your Jazz Blues

Lick #49

DANIELE GOTTARDO – JAZZY BLUES LICK 9

In this final bebop lick, Gottardo plays over the first five measures of the 12-bar jazz-blues form in F. Throughout, blue notes like the flatted third (Ab) or flatted seventh (Eb) over the F6/9 chord lend a strong bluesy vibe, while for the Cm7 chord, the upper notes of a Cm9 arpeggio (C Eb G Bb D) keep the example grounded in jazz.

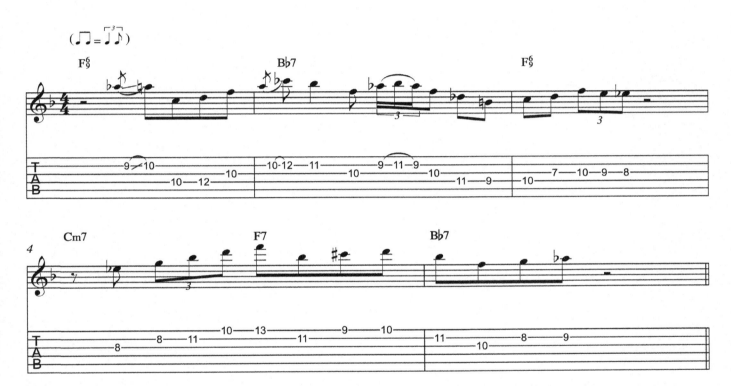

After you have learned these several licks played by Gottardo, it would be prudent to memorize a few of the moves that catch your ear. Mixing bebop lines with pentatonic ideas is an excellent way to develop compelling solos—and one that listeners will certainly appreciate.

Artist:	Daniele Gottardo
Key:	F
Tempo:	130 BPM
Level:	6/10
Course:	20 Licks to Expand Your Jazz Blues

DENNY ILETT – JAZZY BLUES LICK 10

In a different—and more traditional—direction, Ilett, wielding an Epiphone archtop, begins the lick below in the key of G minor by superimposing a Dbmaj9 (Db F Ab C Eb) arpeggio on the Eb9 chord. The rhythms here might be a bit difficult, so be sure to count them carefully and isolate any areas that at first feel uncomfortable.

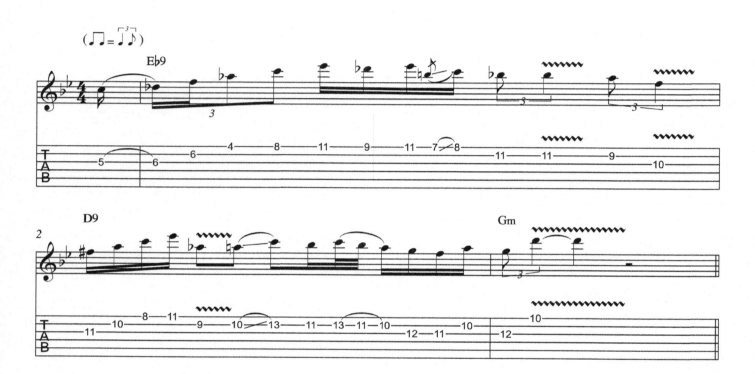

In the second measure, Ilett acknowledges the D9 chord by playing its third (F#) squarely on the downbeat. Note the surprising appearance of the flatted fifth (Ab) on beat 2, highlighted with vibrato, then resolved by the natural fifth on the "and" of that beat. Ilett concludes the lick on a simpler and more consonant note, playing the root (G) and then the fifth (D) of the Gm chord.

Artist:	Denny Ilett
Key:	Gm
Tempo:	73 BPM
Level:	5/10
Course:	Jazzin' the Blues

Chapter 5
ACOUSTIC BLUES LICKS

The steel-string is one of the original blues instruments, and guitarists like Robert Johnson and Charley Patton did much to popularlize its use. While the acoustic licks in this chapter are of the modern variety, they retain the spirit of those pioneers and serve as good templates for how to approach the instrument.

Lick #51

JAMES GRAYDON – ACOUSTIC BLUES LICK 1

While the licks in this chapter all sound great on a steel-string acoustic, as James Graydon demonstrates in the accompanying video, they also work quite well on the electric guitar. For the first lick, over a slow blues groove in E major, Graydon starts in an E minor pentatonic (E G A B D) box in bar 1, then moves to the scale in 12th position in the following measure. Note how the use of 16th-note sextuplets builds excitement there.

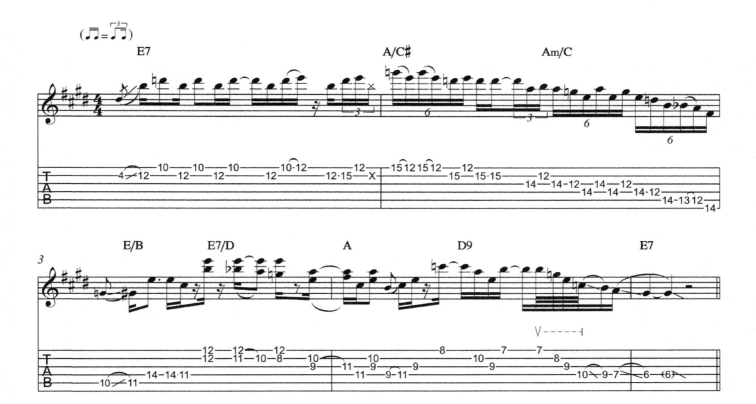

In the last two measures, Graydon varies his approach. Note the tasteful, obliquely moving double stops in bar 3 and the jazzy backwards rake in bar 4, where Graydon plays a Cmaj7 arpeggio (C E G B) over the D9 chord (D F# A C E).

Artist:	James Graydon
Key:	E
Tempo:	82 BPM
Level:	7/10
Course:	20 Acoustic Jazzy Blues Licks

Lick #52

JAMES GRAYDON – ACOUSTIC BLUES LICK 2

Here's another great lick based on the same chord progression as the previous example. Graydon starts things off with some broken major and minor sixths on strings 1 and 3, played in descending order over the E7 chord.

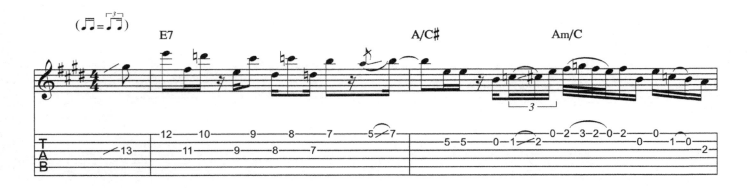

Working his way down the fretboard, Graydon arrives at a passage that makes great use of the open strings, for a country-blues sort of vibe. Especially cool is how in bar 3 he pulls off the the open E string, then sounds the open B, providing a brilliantly ringing effect.

Artist:	James Graydon
Key:	E
Tempo:	82 BPM
Level:	7/10
Course:	20 Acoustic Jazzy Blues Licks

Lick #53

JAMES GRAYDON – ACOUSTIC BLUES LICK 3

Sticking with the established progression, Graydon begins this variation within the 12th position of the E minor pentatonic scale (E G A B D)—a fretboard region that's of course more commonly used on the electric guitar than the acoustic, but which works well on a steel-string with a cutaway. The key to nailing this lick is rhythmic precision, especially when it comes to the rests in the second measure.

Graydon mixes things up starting in the third bar, landing squarely on the E/B chord's third (G#) and then moving up chromatically on the fifth string while maintaining the 14th-fret E on the fouth string. He ends the lick with some more of those slliding sixths, this time all major and moving up in whole steps—another great move for your arsenal.

Artist:	James Graydon
Key:	E
Tempo:	82 BPM
Level:	7/10
Course:	20 Acoustic Jazzy Blues Licks

Lick #54

Track 54

JAMES GRAYDON – ACOUSTIC BLUES LICK 4

This lick over the same progression has a nicely organic sense of development. In the first bar, Graydon explores octaves; he does the same in the following measure but plays them broken. He switches direction in the third measure, with a cool idea pitting pull-offs to the open E string against the fifth-fret E on string 2, then closes things out with sliding sixths flanked by the occasional high E.

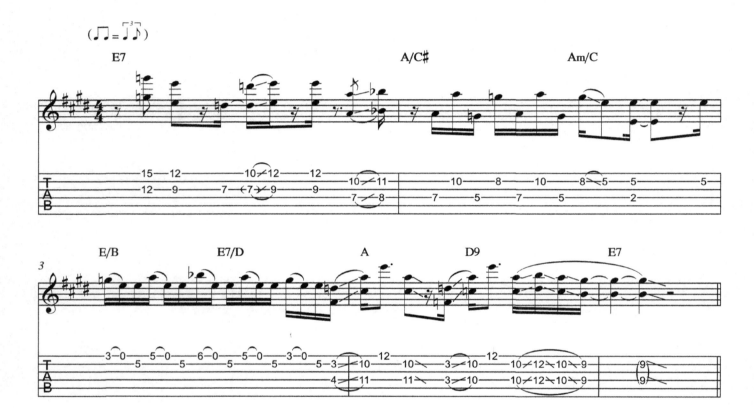

Thinking compositionally like this will work wonders for making your music more engaging, whether you're playing a simple pentatonic lick, a solo over the 12-bar form, or something farther afield.

Artist:	James Graydon
Key:	E
Tempo:	82 BPM
Level:	7/10
Course:	20 Acoustic Jazzy Blues Licks

Lick #55

JAMES GRAYDON – ACOUSTIC BLUES LICK 5

Moving to a different groove and progression, this chapter's last lick has a bluesy, neo-soul vibe. Graydon kicks off the proceedings by playing triads (Am, G, Em, and D) within the A Dorian mode (A B C D E F# G) over the i chord (Am7). He then moves to some tasty double stops for the Bm7–Bbm7 progression.

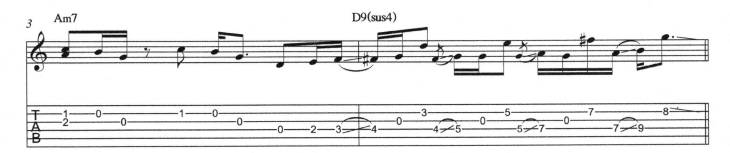

Graydon makes excellent use of the open strings in the last two bars. Note how he plays broken sixths against the ringing open G string to negotiate the D9(sus4) chord. Not only does this produce a beautiful textural effect, it also lends harmonic sophistication to the lick.

Artist:	James Graydon
Key:	Am
Tempo:	82 BPM
Level:	7/10
Course:	20 Acoustic Jazzy Blues Licks

Chapter 7
CONTEMPORARY BLUES LICKS

It might go without saying, but ideally any blues guitarist playing today should have at their disposal both historic and contemporary licks—those drawing from influences outside of the genre, from pop to neo-soul. This chapter explores a bunch of great modern licks, covering a wide range of techniques and approaches.

Lick #56

KIRK FLETCHER - CONTEMPORARY BLUES LICK 1

Here's a smart contemporary blues lick by Kirk Fletcher that works quite nicely on a solidbody electric guitar through an amp on a high-gain setting. It's pretty straightforward, culled mostly from the A minor pentatonic scale (A C D E G), starting in the tenth-position box on the top three strings.

In the second measure, Fletcher works his way down to the fifth position of the scale, remaining there until shifting lower to grab the root note (A) at the third fret. He ends the lick with a dramatic slide to an indeterminate pitch up the neck—the sort of move that is always commands attention.

Artist:	Kirk Fletcher
Key:	Am
Tempo:	165 BPM
Level:	6/10
Course:	Blues: Let's Get Started - 20 Licks

77

KIRK FLETCHER - CONTEMPORARY BLUES LICK 2

For a great bend exercise, try this lick by Fletcher, which starts off with a rapid bend-and-release move between the notes F# and G. Be sure not to over-bend the notes here and throughout; this can be easy to do, especially if you use light guage strings.

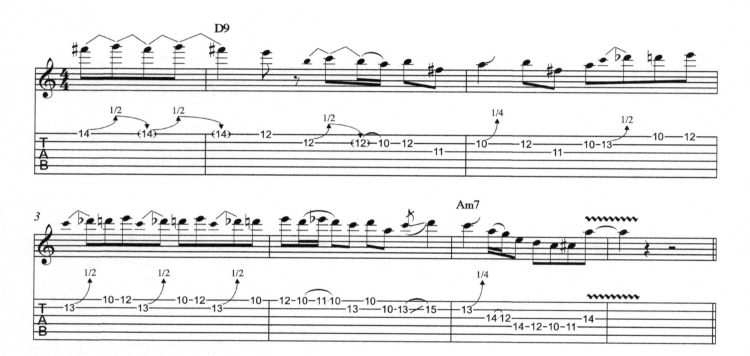

While overall Fletcher's lines here have a distinctly minor character, in the penultimate measure, the guitarist sneaks in a C#, the major third of the underlying harmony. This subtle detail highlights the blue's push and pull between the minor and the major modes.

Artist:	Kirk Fletcher
Key:	Am
Tempo:	165 BPM
Level:	6/10
Course:	Blues: Let's Get Started - 20 Licks

KIRK FLETCHER – CONTEMPORARY BLUES LICK 3

In this killer lick, Fletcher shreds over a chromatically descending turnaround in the key of A minor, showing how you can make the most of the four notes (G, A, C, and D, excluding bends) found in the tenth position of the A minor pentatonic box.

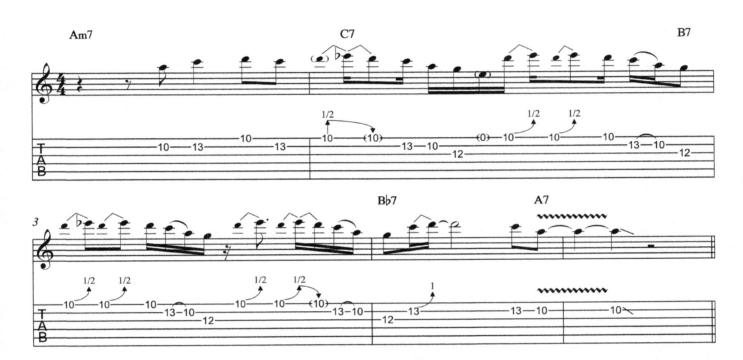

The lick, which is not just fast but requires first-finger bends, is formidable to play at tempo, so take your time in learning it, striving for accuracy both in terms of pitch and rhythm. It's also important to play the lick with total precision, as any kind of sloppiness will not work here.

Artist:	Kirk Fletcher
Key:	Am
Tempo:	165 BPM
Level:	6/10
Course:	Blues: Let's Get Started - 20 Licks

Lick #59

KIRK FLETCHER – CONTEMPORARY BLUES LICK 4

This next lick should be a bit easier than the previous one—but no less soulful. Key to playing it successfully is nailing both the pitch and the timing of the bends in the first two measures, which all fall along the second string. If needed, for the wide first bend, use the 20th-fret G on string 2 as a reference pitch for the bend.

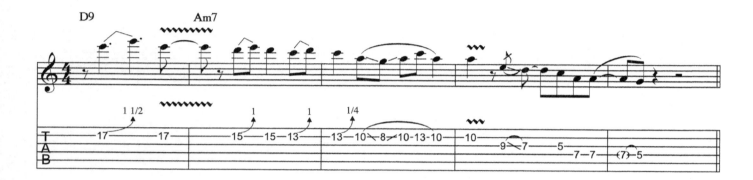

Heads up, too, on the fleeting legto move in the third measure, which may take some preplanning to play smoothly. Use your first finger to slide between the tenth-fret A and the eighth-fret G, and hammer on the 13th-fret C with your fourth or third finger.

Artist:	Kirk Fletcher
Key:	Am
Tempo:	165 BPM
Level:	5/10
Course:	Blues: Let's Get Started - 20 Licks

KIRK FLETCHER – CONTEMPORARY BLUES LICK 5

Here's another relatively easy but very useful lick from Fletcher, culled exclusively from the A minor pentatonic scale (A C D E G). The beauty of this example is that it clearly shows how to switch between three different positons of the scale, thus helping you visualize where it falls on the fretboard.

As before, carefully choose your fret-hand fingerings here. In measure 2, for instance, if you slide between the ninth-fret E and seventh-fret D with your third finger, you'll be in good position to play the fifth-fret C with your first finger. In blues guitar playing, as in life, it's often all about thinking ahead.

Artist:	Kirk Fletcher
Key:	Am
Tempo:	165 BPM
Level:	4/10
Course:	Blues: Let's Get Started - 20 Licks

KIRK FLETCHER – CONTEMPORARY BLUES LICK 6

This next lick is conceptually similar to the previous example. It, too, is based entirely on A minor pentatonic, but moves through the scale in several different positions in ascending, rather then descending order and is a bit longer. It falls nicely under the fingers and gives you a good opportunity to get a further feel for the scale and its most commonly used fretboard locations.

In bars 4–5, note the held root note (A), inflected with vibrato. Playing a long tone at the end of a more active phrase is a great way to add balance and variety to your blues licks while giving your hands a little break.

Artist:	Kirk Fletcher
Key:	Am
Tempo:	165 BPM
Level:	5/10
Course:	Blues: Let's Get Started - 20 Licks

KIRK FLETCHER – CONTEMPORARY BLUES LICK 7

Sometimes it's good to show off one's blues chops, and other times it's preferable just to hold back. With this lick, Fletcher takes the latter approach, interspersing short and simple phrases with relatively long stretches of rest—mostly within the confines of the A minor pentatonic scale.

Using Fletcher's lick as an example, try playing your own minor pentatonic solo over a simple vamp, alternating two-bar phrases with measures of rest. Play fewer notes than you are typically inclined to, and see how that sounds and feels.

Artist:	Kirk Fletcher
Key:	Am
Tempo:	165 BPM
Level:	4/10
Course:	Blues: Let's Get Started - 20 Licks

Lick #63

Track 63

KIRK FLETCHER – CONTEMPORARY BLUES LICK 8

In this lick, Fletcher revisits the chromatically descending chord progression from Lick 58 and solos over it using notes from the A minor pentatonic scale (A C D E G). As with many of the other licks, Fletcher gets maximum mileage from the scale here, connecting its different fretboard positions in fresh and interesting ways.

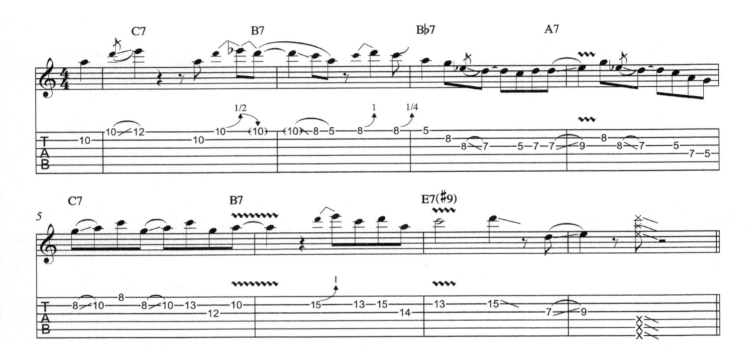

Most of the fingerings should be straightforward here, but heads up on the half-step bend in the first full measure. Use your third finger for the bend (refinforced by your other available fretting fingers on the same string), and after you release it, slide down to the eighth-fret C, while preparing your first finger to stop the fifth-fret A in anticipation of the following pull-off.

Artist: Kirk Fletcher
Key: Am
Tempo: 165 BPM
Level: 5/10
Course: Blues: Let's Get Started - 20 Licks

KIRK FLETCHER – CONTEMPORARY BLUES LICK 9

Here's a blistering modern blues lick from Fletcher, which is built entirely from notes within the A minor pentatonic scale (A C D E G). The lick starts high up on the neck, in a 15th-fret box, and works its way down to the minor third (C) at the eighth fret of the low E string.

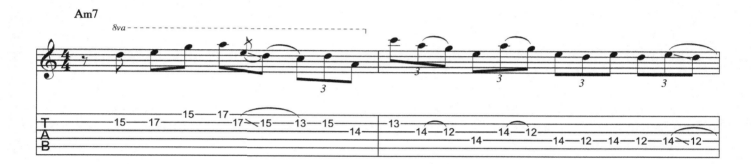

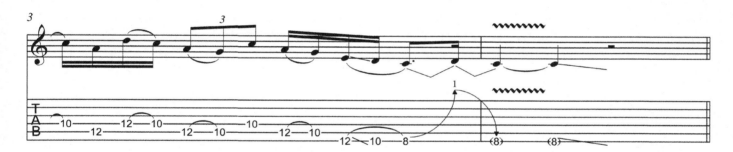

Though much of the lick is based on eighth-note triplets, there are a couple groups of four 16th notes thrown in the mix. If you find it hard to switch between the triplets and 16ths, before you learn the lick, try setting a metronome to a low tempo, and, using a single note, work on alternating between the two rhythms until this feels natural.

Artist:	Kirk Fletcher
Key:	Am
Tempo:	165 BPM
Level:	5/10
Course:	Blues: Let's Get Started - 20 Licks

GUTHRIE GOVAN – CONTEMPORARY BLUES LICK 10

This shredful contemporary blues lick is perhaps the most formidable in this book, requiring a high level of technical proficiency on the guitar and a strong rhythmic sense. It's best to learn the solo, which is in the key of D minor, in discrete chunks before combining them.

Start with the first two bars, which feature screaming bends at the fretboard's upper edge. It's crucially important to play these perfectly in tune, and in precise, syncopated rhythms. Even though this portion is slower than the rest of the lick, make sure that you have it down before proceeding. It's a commanding opening statement that's important for setting the tone of the lick.

In bars 3–6, Govan mixes D minor pentatonic (D F G A C) and D Dorian ideas (D E F G A B C) for a bluesy feel. With their straight 16th notes, the first two measures of this passage should be easy to handle, rhythmically speaking, but pay close attention to the durations in the last two measures, as they are somewhat irregular.

Measures 7–8 incorporate a brilliant chromatic line over an A7alt. chord. In bar 7, pull offs to the open third string highlight the chord's flatted seventh (G). This passage is largely gestural, so it would work to go for the overall effect, rather than learn it note for note. Things cool down a bit in the last three measures, which wrap things up in a bluesy pentatonic manner.

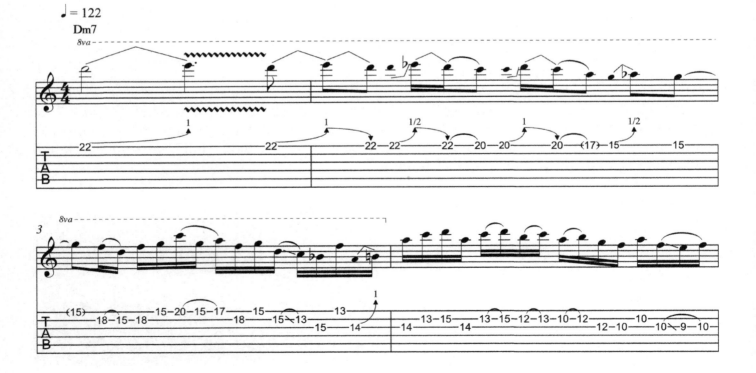

Lick #66

Track 66

JOSH SMITH – CONTEMPORARY BLUES LICK 11

For a change of pace, here's a great lick based on the first four measures of the 12-bar blues in D major, which shows the influence of modern jazz masters like John Scofield. The lick is based largely on the D minor pentatonic scale (D F G A C) in seventh and tenth positions. In the second half of bar 3, the inclusion of the note B highlights the D9 chord's 13th, for a jazzy vibe.

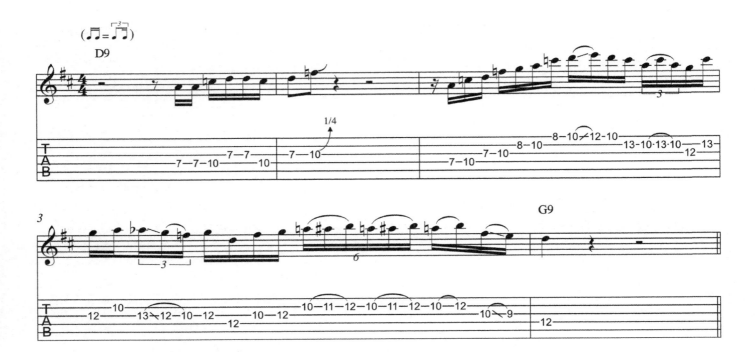

It's important to capture Smith's laidback 16th-note swing feel here. As it's not completely possible to convey this in notation, be sure to closely study the video and play along with it until you can lock in perfectly with the rhythms.

Artist:	Josh Smith
Key:	D
Tempo:	96 BPM
Level:	6/10
Course:	Syncopated Blues

JOSH SMITH – CONTEMPORARY BLUES LICK 12

Here's a fun and funky lick with a strong jazz flavor, which also has a bluesy vibe, thanks to the frequent appearance of a blue note, the flatted third (Eb/D#). With their nonstop 16th notes, the first two measures create a sense of urgency, while the more spacious last two bars provide a feeling of release.

You really need to have your picking and legato techniques in good order to play this lick at tempo. Remember to approach it systematically, slowing down and working things out beat by beat and measure by measure before trying to pull the whole thing off with the same strong sense of groove that Smith demonstrates in the video.

Artist:	Josh Smith
Key:	C
Tempo:	136 BPM
Level:	6/10
Course:	Syncopated Blues

Chapter 8
BLUES TURNAROUND LICKS

The licks in this chapter explore turnarounds, typically found at the end of 12-bar blues progressions. A turnaround serves as a transitional element that leads the listener back to the beginning of the form. Characterized by distinctive chord changes, the turnaround adds tension and resolution, contributing to the characteristic sound of blues music.

Lick #68

GUTHRIE GOVAN – BLUES TURNAROUND LICK 1

Like Lick 65, this first example, by Guthrie Govan, is not for the faint of heart. Tremendous technique and musical depth are needed in order to play it accurately and convincingly. The lick starts off with an attention-commanding, wide oblique bend—the 12th-fret E stays in place while the B underneath is bent a minor third, to D, before both notes are slid down the neck. If this type of bend is not yet in your arsenal, be sure to practice it to perfection.

The rest of the lick features forbiddingly fast lines—especially the tuplets of nine 32nd notes. You don't necessarily have to learn the whole solo in order to get a lot of mileage from it—just choose the parts you find most satisfying, and you can repurpose them in your own blues soloing, whether playing over a dominant seventh chord or a full turnaround.

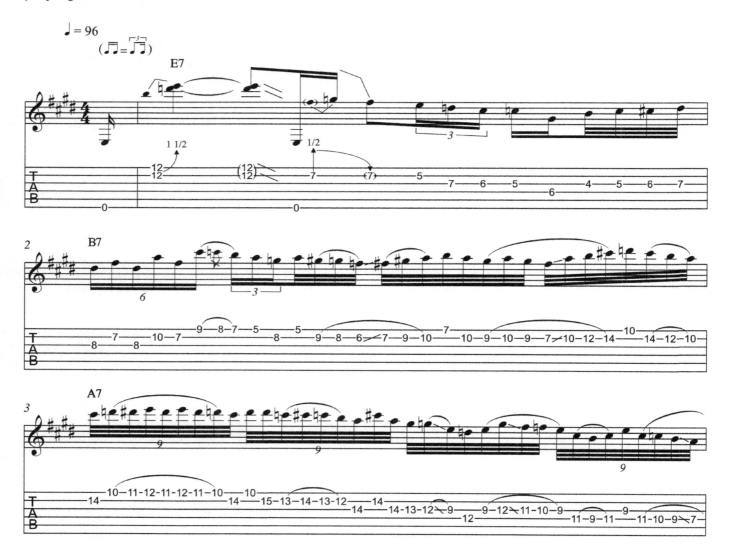

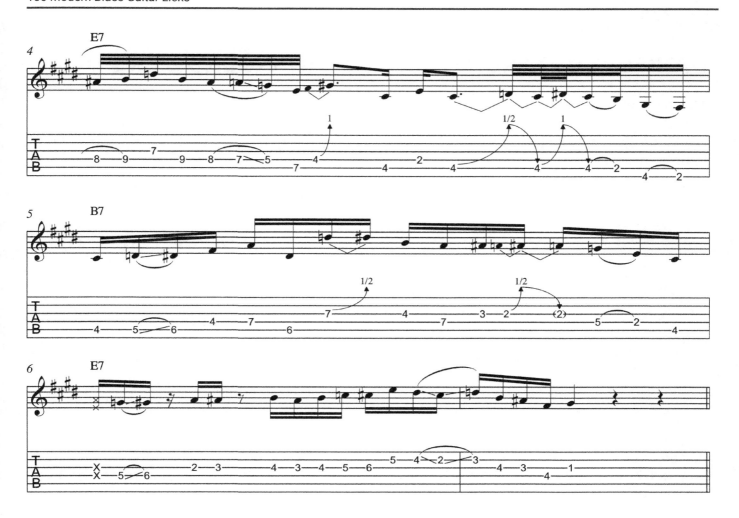

Lick #69

Track 69

DANIELE GOTTARDO – BLUES TURNAROUND LICK 2

This lick by Daniele Gottardo is based on the last four measures of the 12-bar jazz-blues form in F major. While the turnaround technically occurs in the last two measure with the I–VI–ii–V (F6/9– D7–Gm7–C7) progression, the example shows how you might approach this phrase in a classic bebop–informed manner.

Note the use of spicy chromatic notes, like the major seventh (F#) over the Gm7 chord and the flatted ninth (Db) on the C7 chord. Feel free to mix in alterations like that not just when playing jazz but in any kind of blues situation, to enliven passages played primarily using the usual pentatonic scales.

Artist:	Daniele Gottardo
Key:	F
Tempo:	130 BPM
Level:	5/10
Course:	20 Licks to Expand Your Jazz Blues

Lick #70

ARTUR MENEZES – BLUES TURNAROUND LICK 3

Here's a particularly fun turnaround in the horn-approved key of Bb major that is taken at a moderate swing tempo. As Artur Menezes demonstrates in the accompanying video, it sounds terrific on a thinline electric like a Gibson ES-335, with a hint of grit dialed in on the amp.

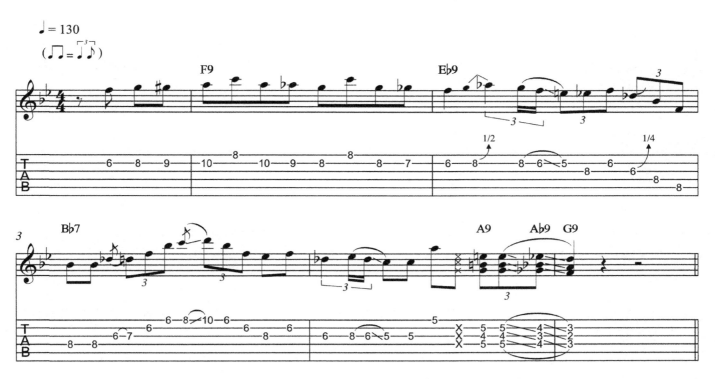

Note the jazzy use of chromatic passing tones, like the G# in the pickup measure and the Ab and Gb in the first full measure. Menezes treats the Bb chord to the sort of formation heard often in jazz and blues, and brings the lick to a surprising place at the end, sliding down chromatically from a compact A9 chord to G9. Make sure that this ninth shape is in your chord library, as it's very handy for any major-key blues situation.

Artist:	Artur Menezes
Key:	Bb
Tempo:	130 BPM
Level:	6/10
Course:	Keep Pushing Blues

Lick #71

ARTUR MENEZES – BLUES TURNAROUND LICK 4

In this slow groove over a VI–v–i (Ebmaj7–Dm7–Gm7) progression in the key of Ebm, Menezes plays a florid lick that first darts up the fretboard and then across the strings, largely within the confines of the G minor pentatonic scale (G Bb C D F).

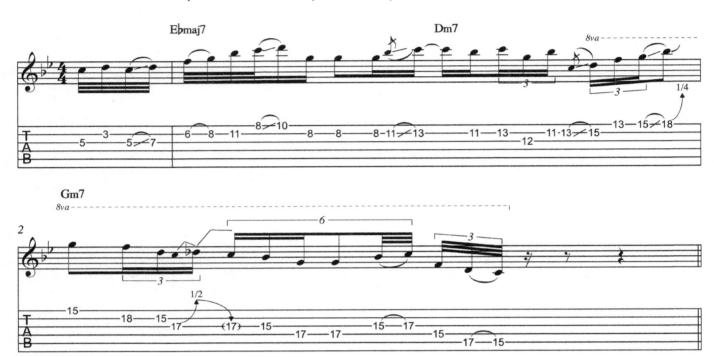

If you would like to play the lick exactly as written, gnarly rhythms and all, then by all means go for it. But it might sound more natural and expressive if you instead try to go for the overall vibe by listening carefully to the accompanying video and then playing along with it.

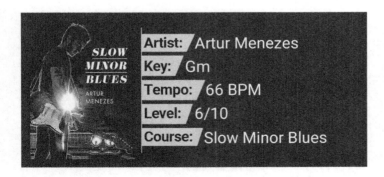

Artist:	Artur Menezes
Key:	Gm
Tempo:	66 BPM
Level:	6/10
Course:	Slow Minor Blues

AYNSLEY LISTER – BLUES TURNAROUND LICK 5

In this emotive turanound in the key of B minor, Aynsley Lister starts off within the B minor pentatonic scale (B D E F# A) in the seventh position, venturing up to a higher box position and then back down again in the next measure.

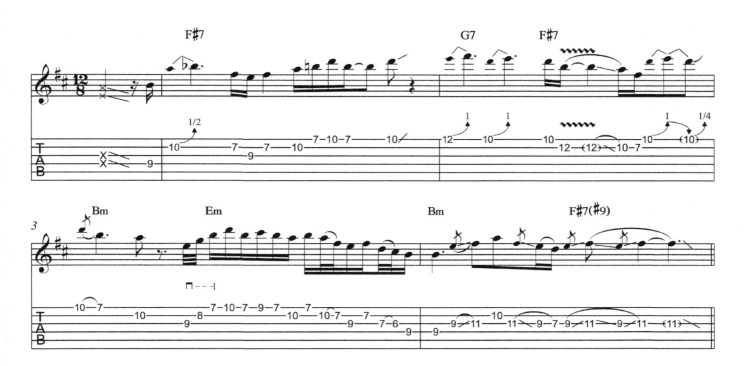

Though for the most part Lister sticks to scalar lines, he does sneak in a little rake of an E minor triad (E G B) in the third measure, an acknowledgement of the underlying progression. This is a prototypical B minor turnaround in 12/8 time, so you might want to file it away for future reference and inspiration.

Artist:	Artur Menezes
Key:	Bm
Tempo:	134 BPM
Level:	6/10
Course:	20 Blues Breaking Licks

Lick #73

Track 73

AYNSLEY LISTER – BLUES TURNAROUND LICK 6

In this B minor variation, Lister also makes good use of the B minor pentatonic scale, but varies his melodic approach, at times targeting chord tones. For instance, in measure 2, check out how he travels straight down the minor scale, beginning on the fifth (F#) to arrive at the F#7 chord's major third (F#) via half step.

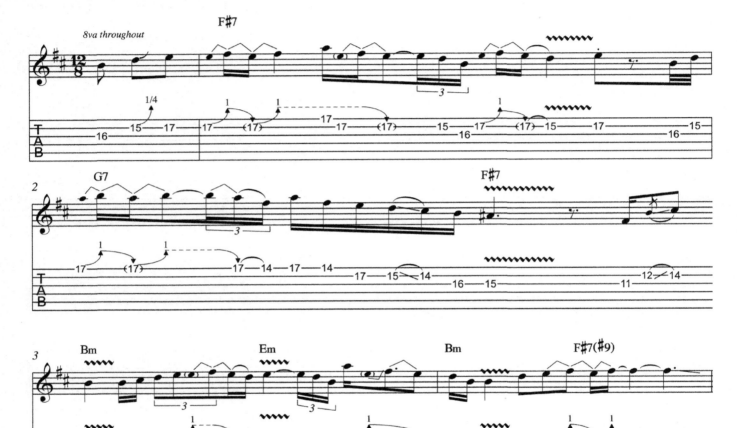

This is another great lick for fine-tuning your string-bending technique—especially the held bends in bars 1–3, as indicated by the straight vertical lines. Remember that the mark of a great blues guitarist is in how skillfully they can bend notes.

Artist:	Artur Menezes
Key:	Bm
Tempo:	134 BPM
Level:	6/10
Course:	20 Blues Breaking Licks

Lick #74

JOSH SMITH – BLUES TURNAROUND LICK 7

Here's a snappy turnaround lick by Josh Smith that will sound especially good on a single coil-equipped guitar like the Chapin T-Bird (Fender Telecaster style) that he plays in the video.

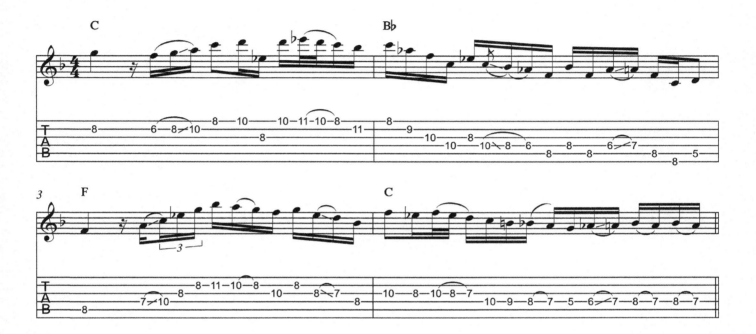

The lick owes its bluesy vibe to the blue notes that Smith chooses throughout—from the minor third (Eb) in bar 1 to the flatted sevenths in bars 2 and 3 (Ab and Eb, respectively) to the minor third again in the final measure. At the same time, chromatic movement like the C–B–Bb–A move starting on the "ee" of beat 2 in bar 4 lends a jazzy effect.

Artist:	Josh Smith
Key:	C
Tempo:	122 BPM
Level:	6/10
Course:	Jamming the Blues: Major

Lick #75

JOSH SMITH – BLUES TURNAROUND LICK 8

In the lick below, Smith plays over a I–V–IV–I (B7–F#7–E7–B7) turnaround in the key of B major. The example has a shuffle feel, is based largely within within the B minor pentatonic scale (B D E F# A), and shows a spare but strategic use of bends in the second measure.

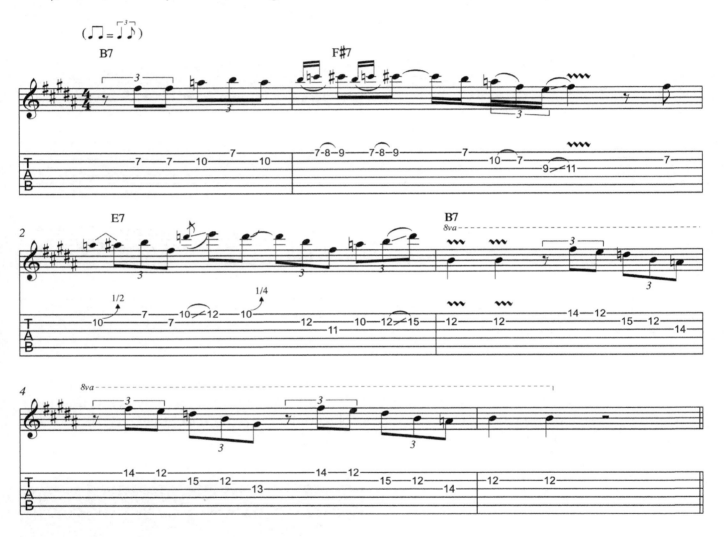

Artist:	Josh Smith
Key:	B
Tempo:	125 BPM
Level:	6/10
Course:	Blues Grab Bag, Vol.3

When he returns to the I (B7), Smith acknowledges this chord by playing the root note (B) twice, in quarters. He then establishes a five-note triplet sequence, repeating it twice before ending on the root, once again played on beats 1 and 2. It's always a good idea to think structurally like this when improvising a blues solo.

Lick #76

JOSH SMITH – BLUES TURNAROUND LICK 9

Here's another blues turnaround in B, this one over an implied V–IV–I (F#7–E7–B7). The lick includes compact, three-note chord voicings on the inner strings, which are great not just staying out of the way of other instruments in a band setting but for providing self-accompaniment in a solo-guitar context like this.

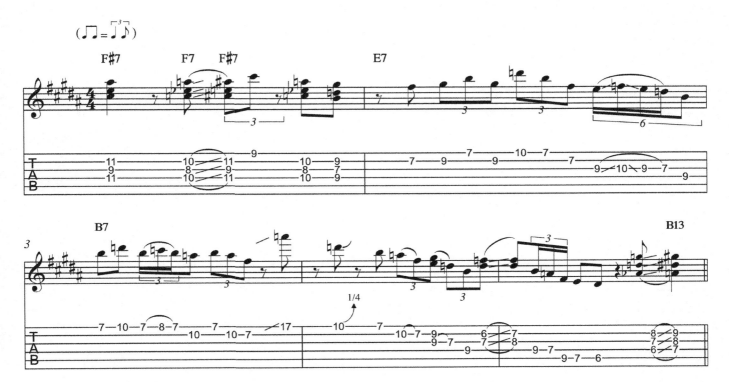

By sliding into some of the chords via half step below, Smith achieves a nice jazzy vibe. Take note of the last voicing, a partial 13th shape, which can be used for the dominant seventh chord in any blues setting, lending a more sophisticated sound than, say, the usual seventh barre chord.

Artist:	Josh Smith
Key:	B
Tempo:	125 BPM
Level:	7/10
Course:	Blues Grab Bag, Vol.3

JOSH SMITH – BLUES TURNAROUND LICK 10

In this last turnaround lick, based in the key of C# minor, Smith mixes blues and jazz concepts in exciting ways. The example starts off simply enough, with notes drawn from the C# blues scale (C# E F# G G# B) over the i chord (C#m7). But the second measure sees the arrival of a surprise chord, the vi minor (Am6), and here Smith plays notes in the vicinity of an Am(maj9) arpeggio (A C E G# B).

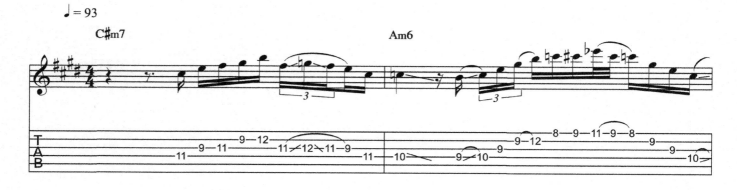

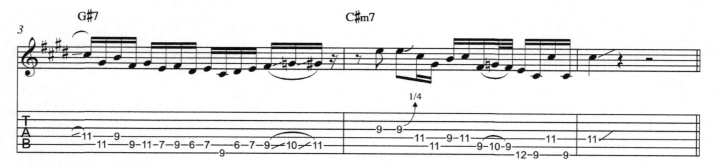

In measure 4, the lick comes to a close similar to how it began—another C# blues line over the i chord. It's often an effective strategy to return to the original idea when improvising a blues solo, or one in any style for that matter.

Artist:	Josh Smith
Key:	C#m
Tempo:	93 BPM
Level:	6/10
Course:	Jamming the Blues: Minor

Chapter 9
OUTSIDE BLUES LICKS

In jazz, an "outside line" refers to melodic or harmonic elements that deviate from the established chord progression or key, introducing tension and dissonance. Musicians often use outside lines creatively to add complexity and color to their improvisations before resolving back to the key. It can be beneficial for blues guitarists to have outside licks at their disposal, as they can generate great excitement when combined with pentatonic and blues scale lines.

Lick #78

Track 78

ARTUR MENEZES – OUTSIDE LICK 1

In this first outside lick, based in the key of A minor, Artur Menezes begins with some outside ideas on the VI chord (F13). By the time he gets to beat 2 of the V chord (E7[#9]) measure, though, he settles into the A minor pentatonic scale (A C D E G), bringing the lick to a close on the root note (A) of the i chord (Am7) for a tidy resolution.

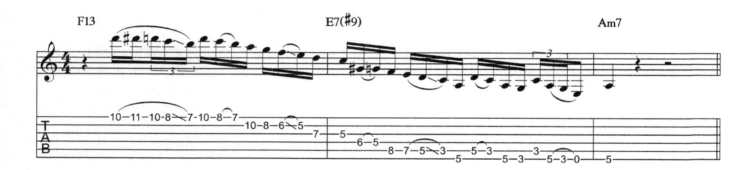

Using this as an example, try creating some of your own licks blending wild chromatic ideas with pentatonic ones, and resolving on the root note or other member of the home chord. Play it—and the other licks here—in a handful of other keys as well for good measure.

Artist:	Artur Menezes
Key:	Am
Tempo:	93 BPM
Level:	6/10
Course:	Keep Pushing Blues

ARTUR MENEZES – OUTSIDE LICK 2

Here's an excellent line that works over the iv diminished chord for a blues in the key of B major. The lick starts off with a straight F°7 (F A Cb Ebb) arpeggio before transitioning to a bluesy line superimposing notes around the I chord (B7). Straight 16th-note triplets give the phrase momentum and require a deft picking technique, so remember to take this one slowly at first.

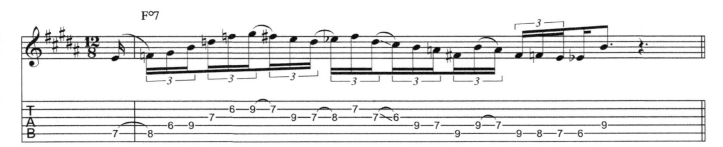

After you've perfected the lick, try using this sort of push-and-pull between diminished arpeggios and bluesy lines in your own licks and solos, as it is a sure way to build tension and excitement.

Artist:	Artur Menezes
Key:	B
Tempo:	156 BPM
Level:	6/10
Course:	Keep Pushing Blues

Lick #80

Track 80

ALEX HUTCHINGS – OUTSIDE LICK 3

In this lick based on a G9–F#9–F7 progression, which can be used on a blues in the key of C major, Alex Hutchings begins with a dramatic bend to the root note of the G9, then hits that chord's flatted ninth (Ab). Next, over the F#9 chord, he plays a cool and useful diminished scale line. Remember—that scale is a symmetrical collection of alternating whole and half steps that makes for striking-sounding outside lines on any dominant seventh chord.

Hutchings resolves the tension created in the first measure with a bluesy acknowledgement of the F7 chord, highlighting its flatted third (Ab), root (F), and ninth (G).

Note: This lick was originally played in fourths tuning

Artist:	Alex Hutchings
Key:	F
Tempo:	82 BPM
Level:	6/10
Course:	Sophisticated Blues

Lick #81

ALEX HUTCHINGS – OUTSIDE LICK 4

Here's a cool outside blues lick from Alex Hutchings, built from a I–IV (Bb9–Eb9) progression in the key of Bb major. The lick begins with the whole-half diminished scale in the pickup bar, and continues to address the Bb9 chord in a wild chromatic fashion. Pay close attention to your picking hand here; it's important that all of the notes sound crisp and clear.

For the IV chord, Hutchings resolves the tension by playing a straightforward Eb9 arpeggio (Eb G Bb D F), using sweep picking to add excitement to the proceedings before coming to rest on a bluesy tritone fragment of the chord.

Note: This lick was originally played in fourths tuning

Artist:	Alex Hutchings
Key:	Bb
Tempo:	122 BPM
Level:	7/10
Course:	Sophisticated Blues

Lick #82

ALEX HUTCHINGS – OUTSIDE LICK 5

It can sometimes be effective for a lick to contain just a hint of outside playing, and that's exactly what's going on in this next lick by Hutchings, which is based on a i–iv (Cm–Fm7) progression in the key of C minor. For the i chord, the guitarist plays mostly notes from the C minor pentatonic scale (C Eb F G Bb), but on beats 3 and 4 of bar 1, he lets loose a torrent of chromatic notes.

For the iv chord, Hutchings takes a decidedly jazzy approach, negotiating the Fm7 chord with an Fm9 (F Ab C Eb G) arpeggio and giving off a bluesy vibe by repeatedly sliding into the ninth (G) from a half step below.

Artist:	Alex Hutchings
Key:	Cm
Tempo:	124 BPM
Level:	8/10
Course:	Sophisticated Blues

Lick #83

JOSH SMITH – OUTSIDE LICK 6

In this lick over an infectious I–IV (C–F) groove in the key of C major, Josh Smith confines his outside playing to the third measure, starting by superimposing an F#dim7 arpeggio over the F chord, which creates an interesting tension.

Back inside the key, Smith wraps up the lick with a classic blues chord shape, which functions as a C6 chord (C E G A) at the ninth fret, but moved down to the seventh fret is C9 (C E G Bb D). The sliding sixth-to-ninth-chord move is definitely a handy trick to have up your sleeve.

Artist:	Josh Smith
Key:	C
Tempo:	80 BPM
Level:	7/10
Course:	20 Licks: Blues Stories

JOSH SMITH – OUTSIDE LICK 7

Over an implied I–V (B7–E7) progression in the key of B major, Smith sneaks in some outside playing in this cool and swinging lick. Note how he inserts a C13 chord in the B7 measure (a technique known as sidestepping in the jazz vernacular), then snakes his way through a bunch of chromatic notes, taking things outside on the E7 chord in the second measure.

Smith resolves things nicely in the final bar by playing a compact E7 shape on string set 2–4, approached from a half step below and taking advantage of both open E strings.

Artist:	Josh Smith
Key:	E
Tempo:	95 BPM
Level:	7/10
Course:	Blues Grab Bag, Vol.3

GUTHRIE GOVAN – OUTSIDE LICK 8

In the lick below, over a static groove on a Dm7 chord, Guthrie Govan works his way down the fretboard and across the strings, along the way hitting a bunch of notes from outside of the key of D minor. In order to best play this tricky and unconventional passage, carefully choose your fretting fingerings, and make sure that the slurred notes sound smooth and at equal volume to those that are picked.

In the final measure, Govan provides a sense of resolution by playing a bluesy bend, from the Dm7 chord's fourth/11th (G) to its fifth (A), pulling off to the minor third (F).

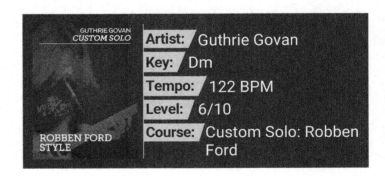

Artist:	Guthrie Govan
Key:	Dm
Tempo:	122 BPM
Level:	6/10
Course:	Custom Solo: Robben Ford

GUTHRIE GOVAN
CUSTOM SOLO

ROBBEN FORD
STYLE

Lick #86

GUTHRIE GOVAN – OUTSIDE LICK 9

In this moody lick in the key of C minor, shortly after bending from the Abmaj7 chord's root (Ab) to its ninth (Bb), Govan ventures outside—especially on the G7(b9) chord, where he includes the major seventh (F#), as well as alterered chord tones like the flatted fifth (D) and raised ninth (Bb/A#).

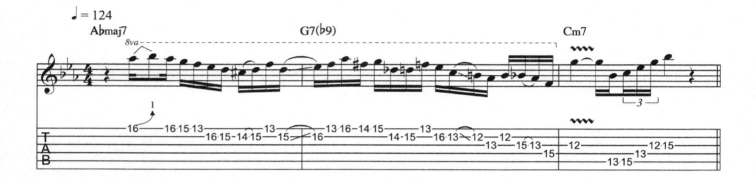

Of course, tense outside lines like this always beg for resolution, and Govan delivers this by landing on the Cm7's fifth (G), followed by a briskly ascending arpeggio of the chord.

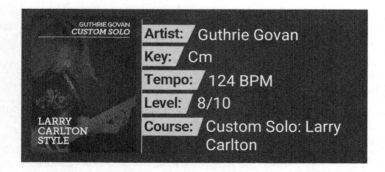

Artist:	Guthrie Govan
Key:	Cm
Tempo:	124 BPM
Level:	8/10
Course:	Custom Solo: Larry Carlton

Lick #87

DENNY ILETT – OUTSIDE LICK 10

This lick by Denny Ilett is another example of the judicious use of outside playing. Ilett starts off the lick in an inside way, negotiating the i chord with an Am9 arpeggio (A C E G B) and then further exploring the i chord using notes within the key of A minor. Similarly, he sticks to diatonic territory for the iv chord (Dm7), with the exception of the brief appearance of the major seventh (C#).

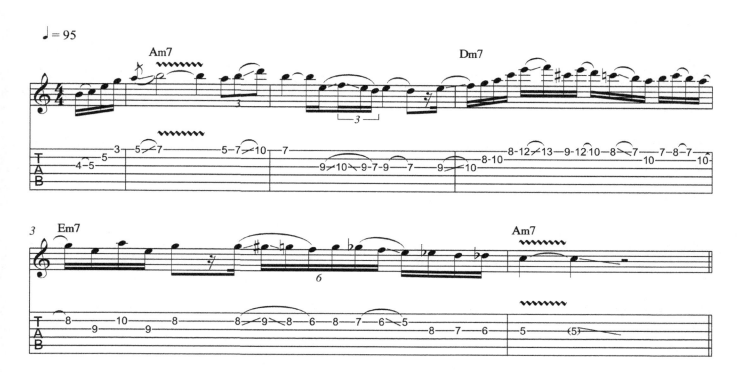

Ilett begins the v chord (Em7) with a simple bluesy idea but then heads into outside territory for the last two beats, leading chromatically down to land on the Am7 chord's minor third (C) for a tidy resolution.

Artist:	Denny Ilett
Key:	Am
Tempo:	95 BPM
Level:	6/10
Course:	20 Melodic Jazz Blues Licks

Lick #88

Track 88

JOHN F. KLAVER – OUTSIDE LICK 11

In this killer lick, John F. Klaver shares an outside technique that makes for attention-grabbing sounds that sound complex but are a cinch to play on guitar. The example is based on a static Bb7 chord. In the second measure, Klaver takes a conventional approach, playing a phrase drawn from the Bb blues scale (Bb Db Eb Fb F Ab) in sixth position.

Then, at the start of measure 2, Klaver plays notes from the minor pentatonic scale a half step above (B D E F# A), creating a wild, outside sound, before shifting back down to Bb minor pentatonic to close out the lick. This technique, known as sidestepping, can work in either direction—for instance, try playing notes from the A minor pentatonic scale over a Bb7 chord, and shift back up to Bb minor pentatonic.

Artist:	John F. Klaver
Key:	Bb
Tempo:	103 BPM
Level:	7/10
Course:	Outside Concepts: Blues Masterclass

Lick #89

JOHN F. KLAVER – OUTSIDE LICK 12

Klaver gives another great example of sidestepping in the lick below, also based on a static Bb7 chord. He starts the example in the ninth position box of the Bb minor pentatonic scale (Bb Db Eb F Ab). Then, in the second bar, he superimposes a B major triad (B D# F#), moving it down to a Bb triad (Bb D F) at the end of the measure.

After that, it's more Bb minor pentatonic with some bluesy bends. Whether you're playing a minor pentatonic phrase or chord shape, try sidestepping to spice up your licks and solos, moving a half step above or below to generate those cool outside sounds.

Artist:	John F. Klaver
Key:	Bb
Tempo:	103 BPM
Level:	6/10
Course:	Outside Concepts: Blues Masterclass

Chapter 10
FUSION BLUES LICKS

Fusion is a musical style that blends elements from various genres, including jazz, rock, and sometimes classical, creating an exciting synthesis. In the context of blues, fusion guitar often incorporates blues scales and phrasing, while expanding the sonic palette with jazz-influenced harmonies and complex rhythms. This chapter includes a bunch of fusion licks in which diminished scales and pentatonic blues phrases commingle.

Lick #90

GUTHRIE GOVAN – FUSION BLUES LICK 1

Here's a punishing fusion lick by Guthrie Govan—do not feel bad if you are unable to play it due to its extreme technical difficulty. In this example, based in the key of B minor, Govan blends B minor pentatonic (B D E F# A) ideas with chromatic moves, resulting in an exciting fusion of styles. Smartly placed bends throughout give the lick a nice bluesy vibe.

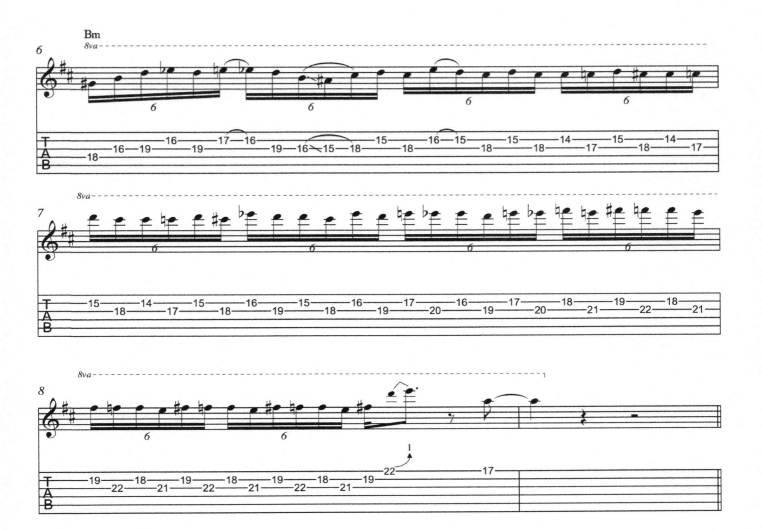

Artist:	Guthrie Govan
Key:	Bm
Tempo:	100 BPM
Level:	10/10
Course:	20 Essential Licks

Lick #91

Track 91

GUTHRIE GOVAN – FUSION BLUES LICK 2

Here's another fusion lick by Govan, this one in the key of C minor. The example starts off with a descending line drawn from the C blues scale (C D Eb E G A) and quickly shifts outside via the use of the Bb minor pentatonic scale (Bb Db Eb F Ab). over the G7(b9) chord.

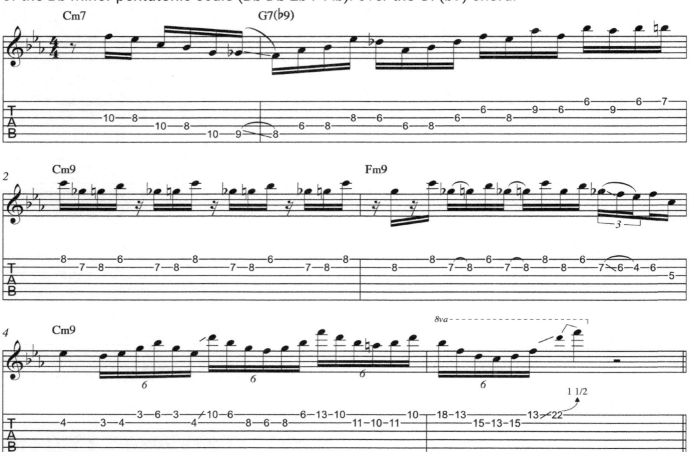

Govan returns to bluesier ideas in measure 2, once again using notes from the C blues scale while developing a motif on the top two strings. He ventures into jazzier territory in bar 4 with some arpgeggios on the same string set, and closes things out with a wide, bluesy bend up to the Cm9 chord's 11th (F).

Artist:	Guthrie Govan
Key:	Cm
Tempo:	124 BPM
Level:	9/10
Course:	20 Essential Licks

Lick #92

LUCA MANTOVANELLI – FUSION BLUES LICK 3

In this cool fusion lick in the key of C minor, Luca Mantovanelli uses fairly straightforward melodic information, but the inclusion of a chord distantly related to the key—the #iv, F#m9—lends an edgy sound to the proceedings. Over the i chord (Cm), Mantovanelli sticks mainly to notes from the C minor pentatonic scale (C Eb F G Bb) and for the #iv, he goes with F# minor pentatonic (F# A B C# E).

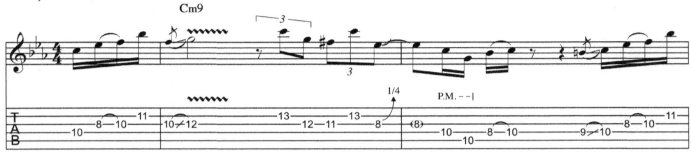

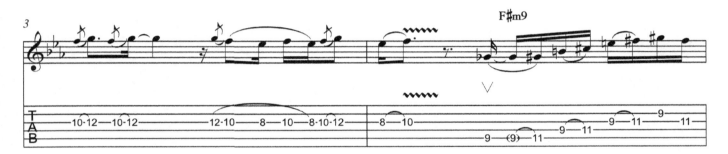

Check out the jazz line that starts at the end of measure 6, where Mantovanelli plays a fragment of an F#m11 (F# A C# E G# B) arpeggio, landing neatly on the root of the Cm9 chord via half step.

Artist:	Luca Mantovanelli
Key:	Cm
Tempo:	100 BPM
Level:	6/10
Course:	Blues Fusion: Beginner

LUCA MANTOVANELLI – FUSION BLUES LICK 4

In this variation on the previous lick, Mantovanelli takes a similar approach, but starts out in the 11th-position box of the C minor pentatonic scale. After a bluesy flourish at the top of bar 3, he switches to the F# minor pentatonic scale, approaching it from a half step above.

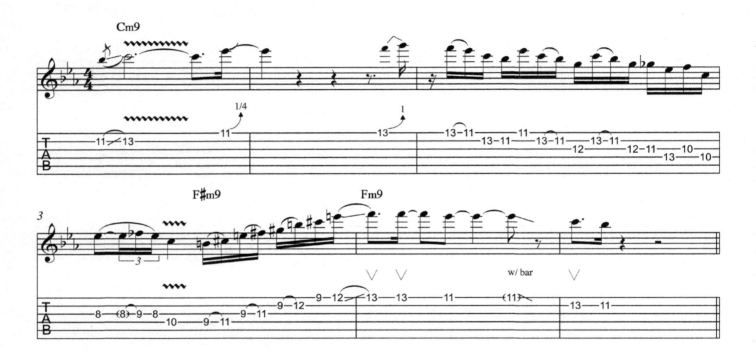

There's another cool half step move between the last 16th note of bar 3 and the first note of the following measure: While the progression descends by a semitone, Mantovanelli moves up a half step to land on the root of the Fm9 chord.

Artist:	Luca Mantovanelli
Key:	Cm
Tempo:	100 BPM
Level:	6/10
Course:	Blues Fusion: Beginner

Lick #94

LUCA MANTOVANELLI – FUSION BLUES LICK 5

Here's a lick based on a I–IV (A9–D9) progression in the key of A major. For the A9 measure, Mantovenelli starts by superimposing a Cm7 (C Eb G Bb) arpeggio, then proceeds with notes from the C minor pentatonic scale (C Eb F G Bb), rather than the usual A minor pentatonic, for an interesting color.

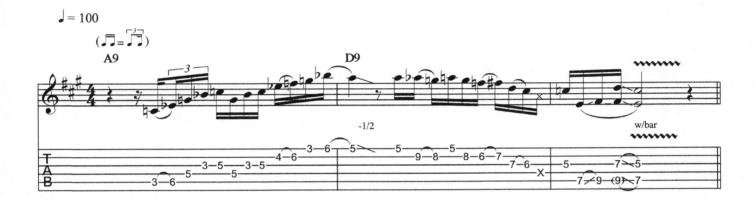

For the D9 chord, Mantovanelli first plays a twisting chromatic line, giving off a modern jazz vibe, and then he ends with some bluesy sliding sixths, accentuated with a vibrato flourish on the tremolo bar.

Artist:	Luca Mantovanelli
Key:	A
Tempo:	100 BPM
Level:	7/10
Course:	Blues Fusion: Intermediate

Lick #95

LUCA MANTOVANELLI – FUSION BLUES LICK 6

Here's a tasty lick over a V–IV–I (E9–D9–A9) progression in the key of A major. Over the E9 chord, Mantovanelli plays a classic blues line that incorporates a minor-to-major-third move—definitely an important one for you to have under your fingers in all 12 keys for any type of blues or jazz context.

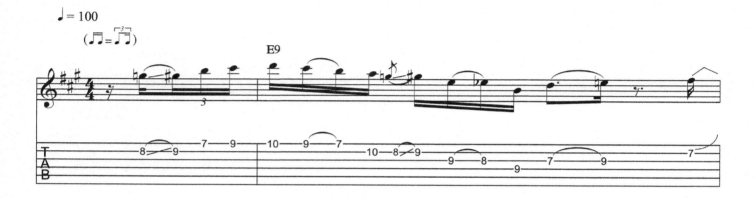

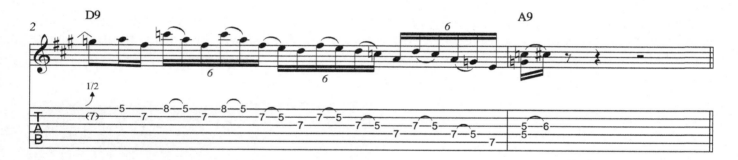

Mantovanelli sticks to the A minor pentatonic scale, with the addition of the sixth (F#) for the D9, in a series of tricky 16th-note sextuplets. He wraps up the lick with another essential minor-to-major-third idea, this time with the A9 chord's flatted seventh (G) underneath.

Artist:	Luca Mantovanelli
Key:	A
Tempo:	100 BPM
Level:	7/10
Course:	Blues Fusion: Intermediate

124

LUCA MANTOVANELLI – FUSION BLUES LICK 7

Here's a lick based on a I–V (A7–D7) in the key of A major that features a nice interplay between inside and outside ideas. In the first measure, after outlining an A major triad (A C# E), Mantovanelli chooses notes from the A Mixolydian mode (A B C# E D F G), leading to the half-whole diminished scale.

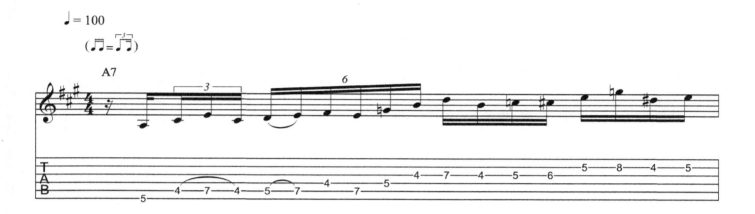

Starting on beat 2 of the second measure, Mantovanelli takes things further outside with some sidestepping, playing notes from within the Bb major scale (Bb C D Eb F G A). He returns inside with a ringing partial D7 voicing, followed by some bluesy bends.

Artist:	Luca Mantovanelli
Key:	A
Tempo:	100 BPM
Level:	7/10
Course:	Blues Fusion: Intermediate

LUCA MANTOVANELLI – FUSION BLUES LICK 8

Mantovanelli begins this lick in C minor with a decidedly bluesy statement, which yields to a jazzy idea: Eb and F major triads in second inversion, played in two different octaves. This works because both chords can be found within the C Dorian mode (C D Eb F G A Bb).

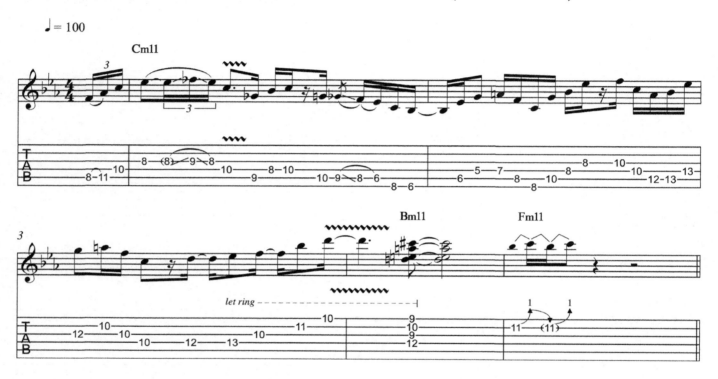

For an alternative to the standard minor open or barre chord, be sure to memorize the minor-11th shape, with the minor third in the bottom, played first as a Cm9 arpeggio and then a Bm11 block voicing.

Artist:	Luca Mantovanelli
Key:	Cm
Tempo:	100 BPM
Level:	7/10
Course:	Blues Fusion: Intermediate

LUCA MANTOVANELLI – FUSION BLUES LICK 9

This lick, based in the key of C minor, begins with a lick that climbs through the Ab Dorian mode (Ab Bb Cb Db Eb F Gb) for the Abm9 chord. The raised sixth (F)—the note that distinguishes Dorian from natural minor)—is never played here, but try adding it to appreciate the mode's distinctive sound.

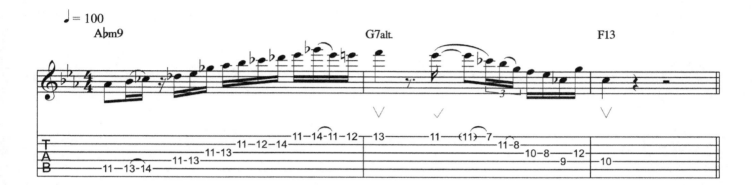

In the second bar, there's a cascade of notes that implies a G7alt. chord and contains alterations like the b13 (Eb) and raised ninth (Bb/A#). Be sure to bookmark this idea, as it's a handy one to have for enlivening a line based on the more common blues scale over a dominant seventh chord.

Artist:	Luca Mantovanelli
Key:	Cm
Tempo:	100 BPM
Level:	7/10
Course:	Blues Fusion: Intermediate

Lick #99

LUCA MANTOVANELLI – FUSION BLUES LICK 10

After a bluesy pickup bar that incorporates both the minor and the major third, Mantovanelli plays whammy bar–inflected moves from the A Mixolydian mode (A B C# D E F# G) over the A9 chord— a passage that calls to mind the work of the late, great Jeff Beck.

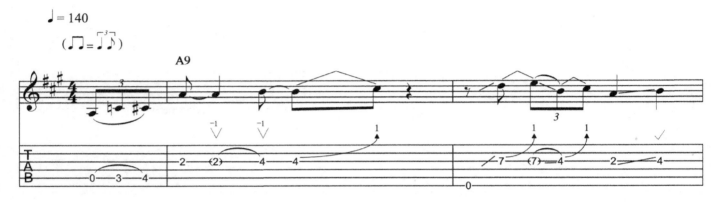

Then in bar 4, in a surprise move, Mantovanelli plays minor third and perfect fourth note pairs from within the half-whole diminished scale—a signature modern jazz move that begs for inclusion in a wild blues jam such as this.

Artist:	Luca Mantovanelli
Key:	A
Tempo:	140 BPM
Level:	8/10
Course:	Blues Fusion: Advanced

Lick #100

LUCA MANTOVANELLI – FUSION BLUES LICK 11

In this book's final lick, Mantovanelli plays some phrases over bars 6–11 of the 12-bar blues in A major. He starts off conventionally enough, playing a bluesy statement within the A blues scale (A C D Eb E G). This is followed by another blues signature move, based around an A major triad shape and ending with a minor-to-major-third flourish—a good one to memorize and play in the vicinity of any E-shaped barre chord.

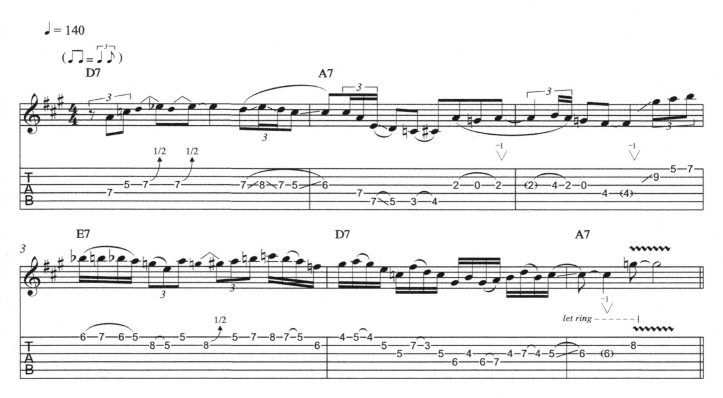

Take note of the altered sounds in the fourth measure. On beat 1, for instance, a C# augmented triad (C E G#) include's the D7's raised 11th (in addition to its flatted seventh [C] and ninth [E]). Mantovanelli ends with a ringing dyad that implies an A7 chord—remember, less is so often more.

Artist:	Luca Mantovanelli
Key:	A
Tempo:	140 BPM
Level:	8/10
Course:	Blues Fusion: Advanced

Printed in Great Britain
by Amazon

41662617R00073